Best wishes from Down Under

Neville Peat

February 2001

WILD
Discovering the
Natural History of a
World Heritage Area
FIORDLAND

NEVILLE PEAT and BRIAN PATRICK

University of Otago Press

ACKNOWLEDGEMENTS

The authors and publishers are grateful for the financial support provided by the Department of Conservation, ECNZ (Electricity Corporation of New Zealand Ltd) and THC Milford Sound Hotel and Red Boat Cruises. Together, their sponsorship has made this book possible.

Title page photo: *Rata trees flowering above Poison Bay.*
Lou Sanson

Previous pages: *Mackinnon Pass on the Milford Track in early spring.*
Lou Sanson

Left: *Endangered species on an island sanctuary. The flax weevil* Anagotus fairburni *photographed on Hawea Island.*
Peter Johnson

Expertise on Fiordland is spread far and wide. For scientific and other advice, the authors are indebted to the following:

Gary Barker, Barbara Barratt, Trevor Chinn, Robin Craw, Brent Emerson, Steve Dawson, John Dugdale, David Galloway, Ken Grange, Michael Heads, Sue Heath, Terry Hitchings, Peter Johnson, Marie-Claude Lariviere, Daphne Lee, Bill Lee, Ian McLellan, Mike Meads, Simon Morris, Kim Morrison, Elaine Murphy, Colin O'Donnell, Ian Southey, Ian Turnbull, John Ward, and a wide range of Department of Conservation staff members, including Richard Allibone, Wayne Baxter, Wynston Cooper, Dave Crouchley, Phil Doole, Eric Edwards, Brian Rance, Peter Taylor, Kingsley Timpson, Nick Torr, John von Tunzelman, Kath Walker, Chris Ward, Dave Wilson.

A feature of this book is the use of photographs from a wide range of sources. We thank the following people for the use of their work: Gary Barker, Rhys Buckingham, George Chance, Trevor Chinn, Wynston Cooper ARPS, Dave Crouchley, Steve Dawson, Tony Eldon, George Gibbs, Ken Grange, Wendy Harrex, Rod Hay, Peter Johnson, Tony Lilleby, Kelvin Lloyd, Rory Logan, Alan Mark, Stephen Moore, Rod Morris, Brian Rance, Chris Rance, Lou Sanson, Lance Shaw, Neill Simpson, Ian Southey, Ian Turnbull, Chris Ward.

Special thanks to Chris Gaskin for his artwork. He was assisted in his fieldwork by Red Boat Cruises and Fiordland Travel.

By the same authors:
Wild Dunedin: Enjoying the Natural History of New Zealand's Wildlife Capital

Published by University of Otago Press
PO Box 56, Dunedin, New Zealand
© Neville Peat & Brian Patrick 1996
First published 1996
ISBN 1 877133 17 5
Cover design by Jenny Cooper
Illustrations by Chris Gaskin
Maps by Chris Edkins
Edited and designed by Wendy Harrex
Printed through Condor Production Ltd, Hong Kong

CONTENTS

1 A Natural Heritage
As wild as it gets *page 8*

2 Rock of Ages
Fiordland geology *page 16*

3 Water World
The Waiau's many guises *page 28*

4 The North
High and mighty *page 50*

5 Fathoming the Fiords
Tentacles of the sea *page 74*

6 The South
Last frontier *page 92*

7 Takitimu and Longwood
Adjacent ranges *page 110*

8 Mavora Country
Going east *page 118*

9 Caretaking
Priorities and issues *page 124*

Bibliography
page 134

Index
page 137

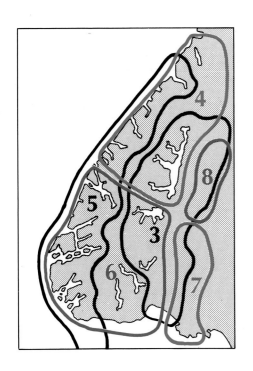

Numbers on the map indicate areas covered by individual chapters.

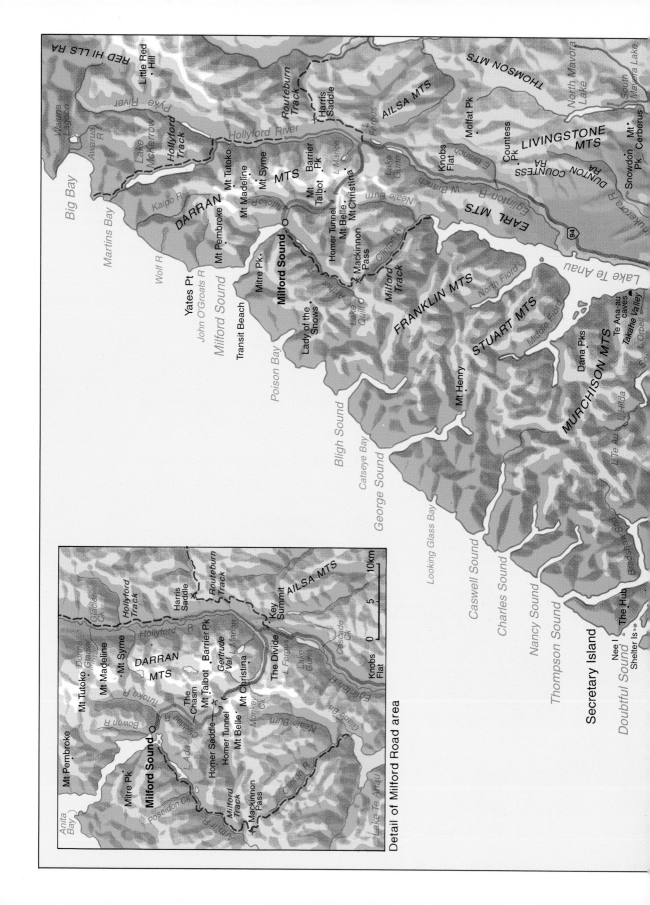

Detail of Milford Road area

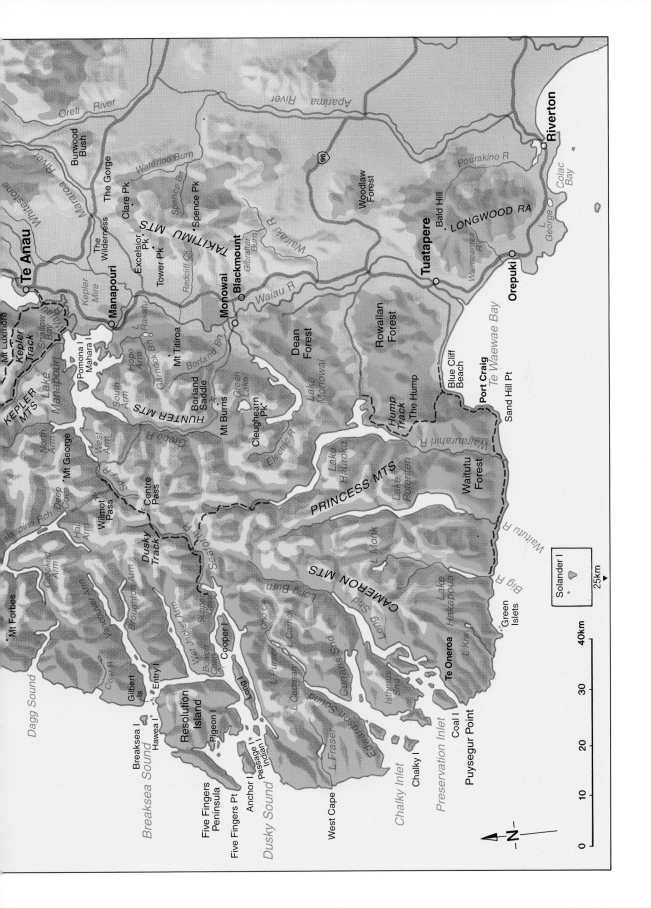

Chapter 1   A NATURAL HERITAGE
As wild as it gets

Left: *Icons of Fiordland (clockwise from top left): takahe, snowgrass, black butterfly, Mitre Peak, fresh-water layer, bottlenose dolphin, Fiordland crested penguin, southern rata in flower,* Dracophyllum fiordense, *and kea.*

In a world largely modified or dominated by humans, Fiordland is a breathing space for nature. It is one of those rare places where humans have made few inroads on the landscape, and where much of the country remains awesomely wild. Fiordland's fascination stems from its high rock walls, valley after lonely valley, its swarming forests and thronging peaks, its diverse water world of lakes, rivers, mires, waterfalls and fiords, and its countless islands. Floods, avalanches and blizzards are the calling cards of a tough climate. This is wilderness on a grand scale. This is heady stuff. The imagination may soar.

To most people, Fiordland is Fiordland National Park, but the park boundaries do not necessarily accord with natural ones. The Fiordland of this book pushes the boundaries north, south and east. This wider sweep takes in the lowlands of Martins and Big Bays in the north and Waitutu in the south, and extends east to include the Livingstone Mountains and Mavora Lakes, Takitimu Mountains and Longwood Range. Thus all of the Waiau catchment is included, not just the western elements within the national park. Nonetheless, the park area is the major focus. Comprising 1.2 million ha, it is by far the largest national park in New Zealand and one of the largest in the world. The bulk of it, too forbidding a place physically and climatically for a network of roads or settlements, was set aside in 1904. Formal gazetting as a national park came later, in 1952.

Only one road – the highway to Milford Sound (State Highway 94) – penetrates the park east to west. Two lesser roads access eastern fringes. From the Borland Valley there is a road (45km) into Lake Manapouri's South Arm. It crosses Borland Saddle (988m), following the transmission lines serving the Manapouri power scheme. The second public road accesses the eastern arm of Lake Hauroko. Its last 6km passes through national park beech forest. To service the Manapouri power scheme, a road was built in the 1960s between Lake Manapouri's West Arm and Deep Cove on Doubtful Sound. This road, unavailable to public vehicles, carries tourists to and from Doubtful Sound across Wilmot Pass. Curiously, Wilmot Pass, Borland Saddle and the Lake Hauroko roadend are more or less the same distance (75km) from West Cape, which is the western extremity of Fiordland (and of the New Zealand mainland).

The Milford road has the only tarseal in the national park, and thanks to the tarseal, visitors have swift and comfortable access to one of the most striking places in alpine New Zealand – the upper Hollyford Valley and Homer Cirque. Glacier-sculptured Homer is all but walled-in. To get quickly to any similar setting elsewhere in Fiordland requires a helicopter.

Much of Fiordland is built of old, hard, crystalline rocks that set the region apart from the rest of New Zealand geologically. The rocks' hard, resistant character contributes greatly to the appearance of the region, for despite the high rainfall and erosive impact of rushing water, the valleys and fiords have largely retained their depth and steepness. As for why the valleys are so deep and steep in the first place, the answer lies in the ice ages and the carving, scooping, grinding power of glaciers, whose story, though much younger than that of the rocks, provides another challenge for the imagination. Instead of the sea, ice once filled the fiords and the inland valleys.

With the retreat of the glaciers, plants and animals could recolonise the valleys from refuges that escaped the ice. Fiordland's plant life contains numerous unique elements. Thirty-five plants – shrubs, herbs or grasses – are endemic to the wider Fiordland area, and most of them are found above the treeline. The endemics include six snowgrass species or subspecies in the genus *Chionochloa*, five herb daisies (*Celmisia*), two trees daisies (*Olearia*), two speargrasses (*Aciphylla*) and two buttercups (*Ranunculus*). A group of smaller endemics occurs on the shores of Lakes Te Anau and Manapouri. No trees are endemic to Fiordland despite the extent of forest in the valleys. Silver beech and, to a lesser extent, mountain beech dominate the canopy, with pockets of podocarp trees occupying lower altitudes and more favourable sites. In addition to its endemic species, Fiordland is home to a collection of plants that are nationally rare and vulnerable to extinction, among them the small-leaved twiggy shrub *Pittosporum obcordatum*, the aquatic stout milfoil *Myriophyllum robustum* and sand milkweed *Euphorbia glauca*. In each case Fiordland harbours the largest remaining populations in New Zealand.

Left: *Endemic flora: The tree daisy* Olearia oporina, *which grows in coastal sites, flowering on Breaksea Island.*
Chris Rance

Red beech forest on the Kepler Track above Lake Te Anau. Red beech is the largest of the three native beech species found in Fiordland.
Neville Peat

The Forster legacy

Western scientific study of New Zealand fauna and flora began in Fiordland when Captain James Cook's *Resolution* put into Dusky Sound in March 1773 and remained there for almost seven weeks. His expeditioners rested and reprovisioned here and scientists Johann and George Forster, father and son, observed, collected, painted and described an array of biota.

As a result, Dusky Sound is the type locality for 18 New Zealand birds and eight fish. The birds include common species such as South Island rifleman, South Island robin and blue penguin, the less common blue duck, New Zealand falcon, New Zealand dotterel and western weka, the near-extinct South Island kokako and the extinct South Island piopio (thrush) and South Island bush wren. Conspicuous among the fish caught and described by the Forsters is giant kokopu *Galaxias argenteus*. They collected num-

erous plants, among them manuka *Leptospermum scoparium*, the tree daisy *Olearia oporina*, the herb daisy *Celmisia holosericea* and seven fern species.

The New Zealand fur seal was drawn and described. It is one of several species whose scientific name honours the Forsters, in the seal's case *Arctocephalus forsteri*.

One insect the expedition could not help recording – and roundly censuring – was the blackfly, better known as the sandfly.

Fiordland's bird world is a mixture of rarity, uneven distribution and uniformity. In the last category are many of the smaller forest birds that are common in forested areas of the South Island and common, too, through much of Fiordland – including bellbird, South Island tomtit, South Island rifleman, silvereye and grey warbler. Fiordland's best-known endangered bird is the takahe, a ground bird, large and colourful, that is found only in the Murchison and Stuart Mountains. The vulnerable yellowhead or mohua is widely distributed in the east, although, like many native birds that fall prey to introduced predators, its populations have declined markedly in the twentieth century. The extraordinary rock wren appears to be holding its own in areas above the treeline, but the long-standing absence of brown kiwis from southern areas, including Waitutu forest, seemingly a prime habitat for them, is a puzzle.

Among the insects and other invertebrates, endemism is rife, making Fiordland an entomologist's paradise. About 350 taxa are endemic to Fiordland in a total count of over 5,000. The groups that contain endemic species include beetles, moths, caddis, stoners (stoneflies), bugs and flies. Many of the diurnal (day-flying) moths are lavishly coloured and patterned – the equivalent of miniature butterflies. Among other invertebrates there are no fewer than six endemic earthworm species, two endemic harvestmen ('daddy longlegs') and myriad endemic land snails. No doubt many new species await discovery because parts of Fiordland are not especially well studied.

The areas with the richest array of birds and insects are the edges or ecotones – forest edge, lake and wetland edges, treeline, valley floor, coastal fringe. Many endemic species also favour these sites. The long-tailed bat favours forest edge rather than deep forest because its insect food is more abundant at the edge.

One of the most dynamic edges is the interface between land and sea. Fiordland's coast teems with marine life. The sea birds and marine mammals thrive here because deep water is close by – the continental shelf is narrow – and food is handy and mostly plentiful. A major ocean current crossing the Tasman Sea from Australia divides on the South Westland coast, with one stream flowing north and the other south past Fiordland and around the bottom of the South Island. Sea birds breeding in Fiordland include long-distance migratory species such as sooty shearwater (titi, muttonbird) and mottled petrel, more local dispersers such as Australasian gannet and Fiordland crested penguin, and the mainly resident species – the gulls and terns. Among the mammals, fur seals are the most conspicuous, with colonies dotted along the ocean coast. Inside the fiords is a different sort of marine world. Here the sea is protected from ocean swells and capped by a brackish 'lens' – a product of the high rainfall and copious run-off. The underwater life is remarkable if not bizarre,

Alpine Fiordland has a large number of speargrass species, including this endemic one, Aciphylla takahea, *found only in central Fiordland mountains, notably the Murchison Mountains.*
Brian Patrick

Below: *Endemic fauna: The spectacular diurnal alpine moth 'Dasyuris' fulminea (wingspan 24mm) is found only in Fiordland and western Otago. It emerges in late summer. The green larvae feed on* Hebe cockayneana.
Brian Patrick

and of international scientific interest.

For its fiords, landscapes, flora and fauna, Fiordland deserves its World Heritage status. Travellers and scientists alike hail Fiordland as one of the world's great wilderness areas, with much left to be explored. A Japanese expedition in the 1980s thought it could find the last specimens of extinct moa in Fiordland, and an American film company in the 1990s envisaged dinosaurs stalking the outlandish terrain. Most people who come to Fiordland, though, leave with impressions of mountain fastness and wild solitude. They can be excused for thinking this is about as wild as nature gets.

Biogeography

Fiordland is a biogeographer's delight. The region is full of surprises and anomalies to do with flora and fauna distribution patterns and associations.

Many species occurring in Fiordland have populations in distant parts of the South Island. For example, there are about 100 plants and invertebrate animals in Fiordland that occur elsewhere only in north-west Nelson – a link explained by the fact that north-west Nelson once lay adjacent to Fiordland and has been displaced by movement along the Alpine Fault (see page 22). The daisies *Celmisia traversii* and *C. petriei* are among the plants that belong only to the wider Fiordland region and northwest Nelson. The true bug *Rhopalimorpha alpina* and the diurnal moth *Harmologa pontifica* are examples of invertebrates that are similarly distributed.

In biogeographical terms Fiordland is multi-faceted. There is a distinct southern Fiordland element in the biota that has strong links with the Longwood Range, Stewart Island and Southland coast. Two species of *Stilbocarpa*, an impressive megaherb, the sand daphne *Pimelea lyallii* and many alpine insects belong to this southern association. At the same time, there is a distinct northern element containing Main Divide species that generally find their southern limit in central or northern Fiordland. In addition, a number of warm-adapted northern taxa run out, progressively, down Fiordland's west coast. A surprising feature of Fiordland biogeography is the presence of elements of Central Otago biota in some eastern Fiordland mountains (Hunter and Murchison Mountains). They include at least 15 plants, 11 insects and one land snail. Many of them are also found in the transition areas – the Livingstone and Takitimu Mountains. The plants in this association include four alpine species – *Leptinella goyenii*, *Kelleria villosa*, *Dracophyllum muscoides* and *Celmisia viscosa*. Two insects are examples – the diurnal moth *Notoreas galaxias* and grasshopper *Alpinacris tumidicauda* – and a large land snail, *Powelliphanta spedeni*.

While climate and topography influence biogeography, ge-

Western weka Gallirallus australis *is widespread in Fiordland and also occurs on the West Coast and northwest Nelson. Flightless and territorial, this robust bird has a wide-ranging diet that includes lizards, snails and the eggs and young of other bird species. It is also known to kill rodents. In Fiordland, the western weka is dimorphic, with a black form and a chestnut brown one. This bird was on the Milford Track.*
Ian Southey

ology has a more fundamental role – especially tectonic history and mountain-building – in explaining the distribution patterns. In Fiordland these patterns form a fascinating mosaic representing five ecological regions and 11 ecological districts. That adds up to a remarkable catalogue of biodiversity.

Mountains of water

Spanning two degrees of latitude in the fabled 'Roaring Forties', Fiordland is the reception centre for the moist westerly airstreams fanning New Zealand. Thus its weather is dramatic, sometimes violent, and subject to change without warning.

Clear calm days are not infrequent, but Fiordland is best known for its precipitation. Westerly or north-westerly winds bring most of the rain; south-westerlies convey snow. Fiordland is one of the world's wettest places.

The mean annual rainfall for Milford Sound, recorded at the village, is 6,267mm. Picture a column of water over six metres tall, the height of a two-storey building. It rains at Milford about 180 days a year – half the year – with most falling in the spring months. Deep Cove, in Doubtful Sound, has a mean annual rainfall of 5,290mm, and the rainfall continues to decline as the height of the mountains reduces towards the south. At low-lying Puysegur Point, the figure is just over 2,000mm.

When moist airstreams crossing the ocean meet the mountains, the clouds rise and cool (about 1 degree Celsius for every 100m), and the moisture in them condenses and is discharged as rain or snow. Average catchment precipitation in Fiordland has been calculated at 4,550mm. The Milford rain gauge set a Fiordland record for maximum daily rainfall on 11 December 1988 – 521.2mm. The deluge was the highest achieved on one day in 61 years of records. The total rainfall for that year, 1988, was 9,197mm, another record.

When it pours with rain in Fiordland, modest-sized rivers become huge in an astonishingly short time. Trampers at the western end of the Dusky Sound Track have seen the Seaforth River swell to Clutha width and stay impassable for days. The rock walls in the fiords and valleys become spillways in torrential rain, with white water cascading right across them. Tracks turn into streams, hollows become ponds.

May to August are the coldest months, but they are also liable to be the least windy. In winter, the valley floors may be frozen all day, and cliffs decorated with icicles. The warmest months are from November to February. Although temperatures may reach the high twenties in sheltered places, the climate overall is cool temperate.

A wet day on Milford Sound. Stirling Falls (146m) is pumping many times its usual volumes and the valley walls above are streaming with run-off water.
Wendy Harrex

ROCK OF AGES
Fiordland geology

Imprinted in dark slate near the entrance of Preservation Inlet are the remains of some of the oldest fossils occurring in New Zealand. They are graptolites – small polyp-like marine animals that lived in surface waters around the world some 450 million years ago. In these Ordovician seas the graptolites drifted in colonies, each polyp fending for itself but reliant on a colonial life, as oceanic filter-feeding 'apartment-dwellers'. When the colony died, it sank to the sea floor. In muddy sediments the protein-rich skeletons of individual animals were fossilised as the mud, over time, turned into mudstone and slate.

The graptolites show up in the fine-grained slate as pencil markings (the Greek origin of their name means writing), usually white or light grey in colour. Of course, the slate must be split by natural forces, mining equipment or a geologist's hammer to reveal the fossils, and in New Zealand the first were discovered by miners in north-west Nelson in 1874. The Fiordland fossils were found in the 1930s by geologists.

Graptolites disappeared from the oceans long ago. Their fossil remains, however, confirm the antiquity of the rocks they inhabit. Whereas many marine fossils have no doubt been destroyed by metamorphism (which involves the recrystallising of parent rock into new types by heat and pressure), the slate, argillite and greywacke of Preservation and Chalky Inlets avoided the worst of the pressure-cooker treatment, and so they are able to reveal life forms from an incomprehensibly distant and alien past.

Graptolites are highly valued as index fossils. They were fossilised in deposits in deep ocean as well as in shallow waters. They occurred worldwise and evolved rapidly. For all these reasons, their fossils provide strong clues as to the age of older rocks.

Left: *Graptolite fossils collected from around Chalky and Preservation Inlets.*
D.V. Weston/Otago University Geology Dept

Above: *Some of the oldest rocks in New Zealand are exposed along the south-west coast of Fiordland. These stratified bluffs are on Chalky Island.*
Lou Sanson

The world map of 500 million years ago is unrecognisable today. Instead of the familiar continents of today and the great tracts of ocean that separate them in the southern hemisphere, there were just a few gigantic land masses. The earth spun more slowly then. The day/night cycle was about 26 hours long. Antarctica, South America, Africa, India, Australia and New Zealand together formed Gondwana (named after a region in India), which started breaking up about 130 million years ago as rifts developed in the earth's crust. The continents of today, founded on separate plates of the crust, began rafting off at different angles and speeds; new seas were created. The Tasman Sea began forming about 80 million years ago as the New Zealand 'micro-continent' – a chip off the old block – separated from Australia. By this time the graptolites were long extinct, but they had left their mark in the ancestral sea-floor muds.

By this time, too, Fiordland's basement metamorphic rocks, including schist, gneiss and orthogneiss, had been formed by untold compression and heat affecting sediments eroded off an adjacent volcanic arc. Gneiss and orthogneiss rocks are granular and often have a streaky or banded appearance – garnet crystals are common in the gneiss around Milford Sound. Schist is finer, more layered and relatively brittle compared to gneiss.

Between 100 and 300 million years ago, from deep down in the earth, molten rock or magma was pushed up into the crust at various places to form rocks of igneous (plutonic) origin, including granite, diorite and gabbro. These are hard crystalline rocks, often speckled in appearance. Granite contains silica-rich minerals, quartz and feldspar. Diorite has black crystals of hornblende and sometimes light-green epidote crystals. Gabbro is a dark rock with coarse crystals.

In the Permian period (245-295 million years ago) volcanic activity occurred to the east. The eruptions, lava flows and subsequent cooling created new kinds of rock, including basalt and andesite, which were in turn metamorphosed. The rocks of the Eglinton/Hollyford area, Takitimu Mountains and Longwood Range originated from this volcanism. Subsequent intrusions added to the complexity, especially in the Longwood Range.

So to the last 100 million years. The area now known as Fiordland (without its fiords, deep lakes and high mountains) had a flatter topography, with large tracts of the land being alternately flooded or exposed as sea levels fluctuated. In the Middle Cretaceous period 100 million years ago, large low-lying lakes and coal-forming peat swamps appeared south-west of the present Waitutu-Preservation Inlet coastline. Dinosaurs would have roamed this region. Rivers carried large amounts of sand and gravel from the eroding hilly hinterland, and volcanoes studded western areas. At times the land extended 100km south of the present coastline.

Pinkish-brown feldspar crystals show up in this specimen of speckled Takahe granodiorite.
Ian Turnbull

Igneous rocks may be volcanic or plutonic. Volcanic rocks have been forced to the surface by eruptions. Plutonic rocks form from upwellings of magma that have not reached the surface but have intruded into lines of weakness in the earth's crust. Although made of minerals similar to those found in volcanic rocks, plutonic rocks have larger crystals because of their slower cooling.

Uplifting story

The story of Fiordland's rocks is long and convoluted, tracing back over 500 million years and involving rocks from all three main categories – sedimentary, metamorphic and igneous. The Fiordland area, lying adjacent to one of the world's major plate boundaries, has been subjected to just about every geological and geomorphological process going – sedimentation, compression, uplift, folding, faulting, erosion, marine transgression and regression, tectonic plate subduction and movement, alluvial fan development, and, not the least, glaciation.

And the picture is changing as new geological studies are made. Fiordland used to be described as a single, if complex, geological block underlaid by ancient basement rock. Now it seems the north-western region is younger than was once supposed, comprised mainly of orthogneiss that is about 100 to 150 million years old. A second structural block is located in the south-west and is defined by the Dusky Fault (running north-east through Dusky Sound and the Seaforth and Spey Valleys) and the Hauroko Fault to the east. This block is decidedly ancient – 450-500 million years old

In eastern Fiordland there is a mixture of orthogneiss and intrusive igneous rocks ranging from 400 to 65 million years old. Limestone deposits, laid down under the sea, are also exposed in this eastern sector, dating back more than 25 million years. Between 25 and 40 million years ago the sea intermittently flooded the area where the Te Anau Basin and Waiau Basins now lie. As with the south-west slate, the limestone contains marine fossils that provide indelible clues as to their age.

The rocks of Fiordland were compressed, folded and heaved upwards in the Pliocene mountain-building era, known as the Kaikoura Orogeny, which lasted about three million years. And then came the ice ages (see page 25).

Earthquakes

Fiordland is a seismic circus. Its mountains constitute a multi-gabled marquee within which fault lines act out the role of ringmasters. The mountains are liable to rock on their foundations. The Alpine Fault triggers its share of earthquakes but not all seismic activity can be blamed on it. In reality, most of the 'quakes are centred deep down in the earth and barely felt on the surface, although several earthquakes measuring over 6 on the Richter Scale were recorded in Fiordland in the 1980s and 1990s.

But the sea struck back. By 30 million years ago, rising sea levels had reduced the land area to an oval island 120km long and 70km wide, ranging from present-day Caswell Sound to Lake Hauroko, with the head of what would become Doubtful Sound more or less at the centre. Smaller islands lay to the north and south. Limestone-forming sediments began to be deposited. Soon after this, about 25 million years ago, the Alpine Fault (see page 22) began to develop and exert a powerful influence on the height and shape of the landscape. The Moonlight Fault was already dominant in the east, together with the Livingstone and Hollyford Faults. To the south, the Te Anau Basin and Waiau Basin were formed from depressions controlled by these main faults and numerous splinter faults.

These large basins are separated now by the Blackmount hills, where the Moonlight Fault meets the Hauroko Fault. The latter angles south-west past Lakes Monowai, Hauroko and Poteriteri to enter the sea near the Aan River, just west of the Waitutu River mouth. Over millions of years, the basins filled with sediments washed off the land into river and sea. The sea occupied the basins till the early Miocene about 15 million years ago. Colossal amounts of sand and gravel built up. In the Monowai area, beneath Dean Forest, the sediments are up to 8,000m deep. Sediments to a similar depth are found in the Te Anau Basin, too.

By the middle Pliocene three million years ago, the coastline was more or less where it is today. But with the ice ages imminent, great topographical changes were in store for the region (see page 25).

THE LIMESTONE STORY

At intervals along the eastern side of Fiordland National Park, limestone bluffs rise conspicuously above or out of beech forest. They represent a discontinuous belt of limestone that extends about 75km from the Murchison Mountains to Lake Hauroko. It was formed 25 to 28 million years ago when a shallow sea covered most of eastern Fiordland.

Water dissolves and erodes limestone. The Tunnel Burn, draining into Lake Te Anau, has created the Aurora and Te Ana-au Caves. There are also limestone caves at a much higher altitude, notably those found above the treeline on the flanks of Mt Luxmore. Trampers on the Kepler Track walk along the base of an imposing set of grey limestone bluffs that loom up out of the forest above Brod Bay, Lake Te Anau. Here the 25 million-year-old limestone is sitting on gabbro, a much harder and older (probably 145 million years) dark-green rock.

Limestone is a sedimentary rock. Its chief ingredient is calcite (calcium carbonate), which is obtained from the hard remains of shells and other marine life. There may be some sand and mud mixed in. Just south of Mt Luxmore a sandy limestone overlays a bed of conglomerate rock, which is made up of cemented boulders, pebbles, mud and sand. This conglomerate,

Above: *Limestone tors decorate a ridge in the Murchison Mountains that would have been under the sea at one time. Lake Te Anau lies below.*
Brian Rance

Above: *A fossilised* Haliotis *shell, ancestor of paua, from near Mt Luxmore.*
D.V. Weston/ Otago University Geology Dept

about 1,300m above sea level, contains a treasure trove of marine fossils. Ancestors of today's paua (*Haliotis*) are found here. There are also brachiopods, echinoids (sea urchins), encrusting bryozoa and calcareous algae. Palaeontologists have also identified a fossil species of *Cookia* that is closely related to today's Cook's turban shell *Cookia sulcata*, which reaches an impressive 8cm in height and 9cm in width at the base.

In fact, all the molluscs in the Luxmore fossil collection closely resemble at generic level fauna currently living on New Zealand's rocky shores. Picture a rocky seashore with turban shells and paua grazing kelp and other seaweeds some 25 million years ago. Then uplift the whole shoreline and adjacent land more than 1km above sea level and you have Mt Luxmore, now more than 50km from the nearest ocean coast, the entrance of Doubtful Sound.

Although Fiordland's limestone or karst landscape is not as extensive or exposed as, say, the karst of north-west Nelson, it does have the hallmarks of karst country – caves decorated with speleothems, sinister sinkholes, soaring bluffs, and fluted outcrops.

Right: *Limestone bluff, Kepler Track.*
Neville Peat

THE ALPINE FAULT

Over the last 30 million years, the Alpine Fault has changed the face of southern New Zealand. A deep-seated fracture in the crust of the earth running from Marlborough through to Fiordland, it marks the boundary between the Australian and Pacific Plates. Leaving the land at Stripe Point just north of the entrance to Milford Sound, the Alpine Fault curves around the Fiordland coast. It is soon deepening the sea. Just 10km off Breaksea Sound, the sea reaches a depth of about 1,800m. Further south, the Alpine Fault is expressed as the prodigious Puysegur Trench.

Off Fiordland the Australian Plate is diving (subducting) under the Pacific Plate, which is being heaved up. The Southern Alps and Fiordland mountains are the result of this stupendous collision. Although the uplift east of the Alpine Fault is measured only in millimetres per year (10 to 20mm is the estimate for the Alps; Fiordland has a smaller uplift), in geological terms it is an express rate. The Southern Alps are less than five million years old and Fiordland's mountains are thought to be a similar age. Their present height was reached about two million years ago; erosion has kept them in an uneasy check since. Given the great age of the rocks and New Zealand's Gondwanan history, the mountains have sprung up virtually overnight.

Then there is the question of horizontal displacement along the Alpine Fault. Parts of north-west Nelson once lay adjacent to Fiordland. The ultramafic rocks of Nelson's Dun Mountain Ophiolite Belt west of the Alpine Fault are the same as those of the Red Mountain area just north of Fiordland, which is east of

Ultramafic rocks

A strip of ultramafic rocks is exposed on the Livingstone Mountains, from South Mavora Lake to the East Branch of the Eglinton. These ultramafic rocks, similar to the belt found at Red Mountain, Red Hills Range and the Little Red Hills in Mount Aspiring National Park, are conspicuously bare of vegetation. The reddish colour of the rocks comes from the oxidising of their iron content. The term ultramafic, derived from latin, refers to the their high levels of magnesium ('ma') and iron ('ferric'). The high concentrations of magnesium and other toxic elements or minerals account for the impoverished plant growth.

Below: *The stark ultramafic landscape on Mt Eldon at about 1,600m in the Livingstone Mountains, with North Mavora Lake in the background.*
Brian Patrick

the fault – and 480km away! This phenomenon came to light with research done in the late 1940s. For a fault as powerful and active as the Alpine Fault, 20 million years is plenty of time for reconstructing a country.

Fiordland's jumbled topography is the product of a plethora of fault lines. Besides the Alpine Fault to the east, the Moonlight, Livingstone and Hollyford Faults have compressed and uplifted land in the north; the Dusky and Hauroko Faults have strongly influenced the south

A staircase of ancient beaches

Along Fiordland's southern and south-western coast is a geological feature of international renown – marine terraces that range as high as 1,000m above sea level.

Although terraces are found from Te Waewae Bay west around the coast to Dusky Sound, the best-known sequence lies between Te Waewae Bay and Lake Hakapoua – the Waitutu terraces (photo, page 97). Comprising 13 old beach levels, this staircase of terraces extends inland for about 12km. The terraces, now mostly forest-clad but harbouring extensive bogs as well, represent sea-level changes that occurred over the past few hundred thousand years. The terraces have formed from the combined effects of coastal erosion and fluctuating sea levels (correlated with global glaciation and deglaciation), superimposed on a tectonically rising land mass. Three terraces formed in the last interglacial (warm period between major glaciations), about 80,000 to 120,000 years ago. Some old marine terraces are also found on hard basement rocks in the Puysegur Point area.

Below: A skyline feature looking west from the boulder beaches of Te Waewae Bay is The Hump, which slopes to meet the sea from a high point at its northern end (1,067m). The Hump is an uplifted block sandwiched between parallel faults. Uplift of this kind is called a horst. About six million years ago the Port Craig end of the ridge was under the sea. The presence of seams of sub-bituminous coal on the ridge speak of a history of coastal swamps and peat bogs and a time when the land was much flatter than it is today. Coal also occurs at Teal Bay, on the southern end of Lake Hauroko. The boulders on the Te Waewae Bay beaches are of extraordinary colour and texture. Some of the mudstone boulders on the beaches contain fossil shells about 10 million years old.
Neville Peat

Above: *These parallel scratches (striations or striae) on smooth bedrock on an island in Lake Manapouri were caused by rocks dragged along by glacier ice.*
Ian Turnbull

Left: *A spectacular cirque in the Darran Mountains – the head of Falls Creek, below Ngatimamoe Peak.*
Lou Sanson

All over Fiordland, at varying altitudes, there are hundreds of lakes – thousands if you count the smallest alpine tarns. Some small lakes on the large valley floors are kettle lakes, which are formed near a glacier's terminus after isolated blocks of ice become buried by outwash gravels and later melt.

GLACIATION

Just over two million years ago, the earth's climate cooled. Snow and ice began building up in mountains world-wide, and sea levels fell. The Pleistocene ice ages had begun.

In the Southern Alps and across the Fiordland massif, accumulated snow filled the valleys with ice and the glaciers linked up to form massive ice caps. All but the highest mountains were submerged by ice.

There were warm periods over the past two million years, however, during which the ice retreated. At least 12 major glacial phases, alternating with warm periods, affected southern New Zealand during the Pleistocene. The last 'big freeze', known as the Otiran Glaciation, began about 80,000 years ago and kept the southern mountains ice-bound till about 10,000 years ago.

Envisaging the extent and scale of the Fiordland glaciers requires a leap of the imagination. The glaciers reached depths of up to 2,000m. The ice was 500m deep as it rode over Key Summit, which is high above The Divide between the Hollyford and Eglinton Valleys. But perhaps the most impressive evidence of the size and might of the glaciers is to be found in the Fiordland lakes, which were glacially sculpted.

Te Anau and Manapouri, the two largest lakes, have been scooped by glaciers to well below present-day sea level. Te Anau's deepest point is 214m below sea level; Manapouri reaches 267m. The ice that created these trenches flowed upwards at the lower end of the hollow, demonstrating the viscous character of ice under great pressure (compared to the brittle nature of ice blocks in a freezer). Of course, sea levels are a lot higher today than they were during the ice ages. At the time of the Otiran glaciation, glacier ice world-wide lowered the sea level by about 80m.

While at their largest extent, the glaciers transported vast amounts of rock debris. It was collected from rock falls landing on the glacier and from rock ground from the valley floor and sides. This debris, ranging from 'rock flour' (fine silt) to large boulders, is called 'till'; the shaped deposits of till are called

Glacier ice, endlessly advancing and retreating, has a colossal impact on the landscape, and there is no better place to admire the earth-sculpting power of slowly moving ice than Fiordland. Look for these telltale signs of glaciation:
- valleys excavated to U-shape by glaciers;
- cirques at the head of valleys, scooped to bowl shape;
- lakes perched high in the mountains, filling excavated cirques;
- isolated low-lying hills worn down and streamlined on their upstream side and steep and craggy on their downstream side (picturesquely called roche moutonnée – rock sheep);
- 'tear-drop' or hump-backed islands in lakes and fiords, the products of overriding ice;
- hanging valleys from which waterfalls emerge;
- moraine mounds in valley floors (as in the Eglinton Valley), representing rock debris deposited by a glacier as it melted.

moraines, which are left at the glacier edges as the ice melts. Lateral moraines mark the position of the glacier sides and terminal moraines show where the glacier advanced to before retreating.

In the middle of the Te Anau Basin, not far from The Wilderness Scientific Reserve, is a geological curiosity – a large boulder, signposted beside the Lumsden-Te Anau highway, that provides evidence of the way glaciers move mountains. It is an 'erratic', carried by the Te Anau glacier from the mountains in the north-west. The rock flour suspended in the river water issuing from the terminal face turns the river a murky green or grey. This effect is more pronounced in Otago, where the rocks are predominantly schist and not as hard or tough as the gneiss, granite and allied rocks of Fiordland.

Rivers emanating from large glaciers inevitably spawn outwash plains of gravel and sand, and the Fiordland glaciers that drained east have left their mark in the Te Anau and Waiau Basins. The farms of the Te Anau Basin are built largely upon outwash gravels and moraines.

As for the glaciers draining west, the largest would have overlapped the present coastline. Icebergs would have calved from floating ice cliffs that met a surging sea. Meanwhile, the fiords were being progressively deepened by thick sinuous glaciers, some of which were over 30km in

Opposite top: *Cloud filling Milford Sound gives an impression of what the fiord valleys might have looked like part-filled with glacier ice.*
Lou Sanson

Opposite bottom: *Donne Glacier, below Mt Tutoko, is Fiordland's largest glacier – a remnant that continues to retreat. The lake at the foot of the glacier has grown significantly over the past 10 years. The 3.6km-long glacier drains east into Glacier Creek, a tributary of the Hollyford River.*
Trevor Chinn

Below: *Landslides and associated fans have formed lakes in various parts of Fiordland, including the Oho Creek Valley in southern Fiordland. Debris from a large landslide separates Lake Purser (foreground) from Lake Carrick. Beyond is Lake Cadman, with Chalky Inlet's Edwardson Sound in the far distance.*
Chris Ward

length. The Milford Glacier's cycles of advance and retreat have left evidence of five old valley floors on the bed of Milford Sound.

Glacial ice has all but abandoned Fiordland now. The only remaining glaciers are small, confined and perched high up. Not surprisingly, the largest are on the side of Mt Tutoko, highest peak in Fiordland at 2,746m. There are glaciers dotted about mountains to the south, but they are tiny by comparison with the large glaciers of the Southern Alps. The southernmost glaciers in New Zealand are a set of three located at about 1,600m on Caroline Peak near Lake Hauroko, the largest of them being only 8ha in area and less than 400m long.

Climate change

Glaciers – and snowlines for that matter – are sensitive to small changes in average annual temperature. One degree Celsius will make a difference.

In more modern times New Zealand temperatures began to rise from the early 1800s, and the aggressively warm temperatures of the 1950s took the greatest toll on the retreating glaciers. Although colder winters in the 1990s have produced a growth spurt in glaciers throughout the Southern Alps, the trend may still be towards a warmer world and thus the outlook is not promising for Fiordland's glacial remnants.

Chapter 3

WATER WORLD
The Waiau's many guises

In Fiordland, water speaks with many voices, and a full range of them may be heard in the extraordinary Waiau catchment – from undertones of gurgling, trickling, dripping and seeping to a full-throated cascading, sluicing, spouting and leaping. There is no better place to listen out for aqua-oratory than in the Waiau catchment. This is because the catchment is extensive, it includes some of the wettest country on earth, and it contains waterways of just about every kind.

The Waiau River itself is in two parts, and they speak with rather different voices. The upper Waiau links Lakes Te Anau and Manapouri – a hearty but short river, translucent green in normal flows, its surface broken by small whirlpools that speak of its impressive volume, depth and flow. From the air it is a serpent, carving a tortuous path through the old outwash gravels between the two lakes, and making the most of its brief journey (14km in a direct line from the Te Anau outlet to Manapouri's Shallow Bay) and its modest fall (24m).

The lower Waiau River used to set out from Lake Manapouri at Pearl Harbour, where it claimed a New Zealand record – the lake outlet with the largest volume, averaging 402 cumecs (cubic metres per second). This lake outlet serves more as an arm of the lake than as the outlet of New Zealand's second-largest river. The bulk of the Waiau's water is diverted through penstocks at West Arm – the Manapouri hydro-electric power scheme. In its upper reaches, the river has been reduced to a stream-sized trickle by a 4.7m-high weir and control gates, completed in 1976 at the confluence with the Mararoa River 10km downstream from Pearl Harbour.

In the 20 years since the Mararoa control structure was completed, the riverbed immediately below it has carried little more than seepage and floodwaters. In 1996, the power company ECNZ reached agreement with interested parties to introduce a regime of compensatory minimum flows through the Mararoa structure – 12 cumecs over five winter months increasing to 16 cumecs over five summer months, with 14 cumecs during the two transitional months. This regime was intended to restore something of the river's natural order. In the meantime, inflows below the control structure have continued to feed the Waiau as in the past. They are of sufficient volume to give the river some substance by the time it passes Tuatapere, 65km from Lake Manapouri and 10km from the sea. At Tuatapere the Waiau River is New Zealand's eleventh largest.

The Waiau catchment as a whole contains virtually every kind of habitat that water is capable of creating – snowbanks, seepages, alpine tarns, string bogs, cataracts, streams, rivers, lakes, swamps

Powerful water

The Manapouri power scheme, New Zealand's largest hydro-electric project, changed the face of the Waiau River's main stem.

From as early as 1969, Lakes Te Anau and Manapouri were controlled and water from the upper half of the catchment was harnessed to drive seven turbines in the largest underground power station in the Southern Hemisphere, at Lake Manapouri's West Arm. After passing through the turbines, the water drains to the sea at Deep Cove by way of a 10km-long tailrace tunnel. A second tunnel of similar diameter (9m) is proposed in order to make more efficient use of the Waiau's water.

A massive public campaign spanning some 13 years – the Save Manapouri Campaign of 1959-72 – was fought to save the water level of the lakes from being raised. An early proposal envisaged raising Manapouri by as much as 25m, which would have merged it with Lake Te Anau.

As a result of the campaign, both lakes gained statutory protection and are operated within their natural high and low levels. Lake-operating guidelines are carefully monitored by the Government-appointed Guardians of Lakes Manapouri, Monowai and Te Anau to ensure natural values are protected.

Right: *The winding upper Waiau River discharges into Lake Manapouri at Shallow Bay, where sediments carried by the river contribute to its shallow nature.*
Neville Peat

Below: *Lake Manapouri. This view towards the Hunter Mountains, framed by kowhai trees, is from the sandy shores of Moturau. A little shag is roosting at the water's edge.*
Neville Peat

and mires. Then there are the lakes' edges and river banks – riparian margins, supporting their own vegetation patterns. The water world of the Waiau, in its many guises, has a lot to say.

Dominating the eastern side of Fiordland, the catchment covers 8,134 sq km. In terms of water volume, it is the second largest catchment in New Zealand. Only the Clutha, draining western and Central Otago, gathers more water.

The northernmost (and highest) point of the catchment is Mt Belle (1,975m) near the Homer Tunnel, 130km due north of the mouth of the Waiau River at Te Waewae Bay. From headwaters under Mt Belle the Neale Burn flows into the Clinton River, which feeds the head of Lake Te Anau. Te Anau's largest tributary, the Eglinton River, has its source at The Divide, which is also close to the northern extremity of the catchment. From this saddle with the Hollyford Valley, utilised by the Milford Road, the Eglinton makes its way through two small lakes (Fergus and Gunn) and a series of grassy flats and forested gorges to reach Lake Te Anau just north of Te Anau Downs.

In the east the Waiau catchment is bounded by the Thomson Mountains flanking Lake Wakatipu, and the Takitimu Mountains and Longwood Range further south. The western edge of the catchment borders on mountains near the head of several fiords – for example, there are headwaters within 4km of Deep Cove, at the head of Doubtful Sound.

Lakes Te Anau and Manapouri are central features of the catchment, pooling the bulk of the water. The combined catchments of Lakes Te Anau and Manapouri (4,483sq km or 55 per cent of the total Waiau catchment) account for 78 per cent of average flows. Both of these lakes (and Lake Monowai to the south) lie within Fiordland National Park, which protects the wetter western side of the catchment. A rainshadow effect is created by the western mountains, with less rain falling in the east. Average annual rainfall in a typical small catchment west of Lake Te Anau will be in the order of 7,000-8,000mm, whereas in the Takitimu Mountains to the east annual rainfall of just 1,000-1,500mm can be expected.

While these largest lakes in the Waiau catchment are within Fiordland National Park, the Waiau River itself lies outside the park. In places, though, it abuts the park boundary on its long journey to the sea.

Lakes galore

Fiordland is as much a region of lakes as it is of fiords. Lakes Te Anau and Manapouri dominate the scene but the southern trio of Monowai (20.6km long, 2.5km maximum width), Hauroko (33.7km long, 7.8km maximum width) and Poteriteri (27km long, 3km maximum width) and the north's Lake McKerrow (15km long, 2.2km maximum width) are all substantial lakes, displaying their glacial origin through their long, narrow form.

Of these 'second tier' lakes, only Monowai feeds into the Waiau. Then there are the smaller lakes of the region. Several hundred are worthy of being listed as lakes. In the Waiau, the prominent ones are also in tandem and include Green and Island Lakes, which drain into the Grebe and so to Manapouri's South Arm; Lakes Te Au and Hilda, which drain into the Esk Burn and so to the South Fiord of Lake Te Anau; Lakes Fergus and Gunn, which drain into the Eglinton River and so to Lake Te Anau; and North and South Mavora Lakes, which feed the Mararoa River and so reach Lake Manapouri (as a result of the weir and control gates at the Waiau confluence).

LAKELAND

Lake Te Anau, the Waiau catchment's best-known element, is the largest lake in the South Island and the second-largest in New Zealand (after Taupo). Manapouri is our fifth largest lake and arguably the most beautiful – a pleasing display of arms, islands and beaches set amongst steep, forested mountains.

Perhaps the most striking feature of these lakes is their similarity to the fiords. In just about any of the arms the surrounding mountains rise almost sheer from the water. Beaches are few. Deltas have formed around river mouths, but for the most part the lakes are bath-shaped.

To add to the confusion, Te Anau's large arms, stretching westward, are mapped as fiords – South Fiord, Middle Fiord and North Fiord. Manapouri has four arms, which are smaller than Te Anau's fiords and named Hope, South, West and North.

Te Anau's maximum depth (417m) is recorded from South Fiord, where ancient glaciers have left the floor unevenly excavated. There is a sill near the entrance of South Fiord that rises to a depth of only 100m before falling away again in the main body of the lake to depths of about 200m. This basin-sill development occurs also in the fiords open to the sea.

Inflows into Lakes Te Anau and Manapouri typically peak in October-December and they are lowest during winter months. In November 1988, following flood rains, both lakes recorded their highest levels since records began in the 1920s – 205.1m above sea level for Te Anau, which was more than 3m above the mean, and 181.5m for Manapouri, which was also more than 3m above the mean. A torrent roared down the Upper Waiau – a record 1100cumecs – and caused serious slumping of the banks.

High winds are liable to whip up furious seas. The longer the fetch, the higher the waves. Waves up to 3m high have been measured west of Centre Island in a north-west gale thundering down Te Anau's North Fiord. Yet mirror reflections might greet a yachtie the next day. Water quality is similar for both lakes – cold and clear. Inflows from tributaries are relatively free of sediment. On a fine calm day, the lake water can be transparent to depths of about 10m.

The water quality has attracted the interest of a number of developers over the years. There is a proposal to export Manapouri water in bulk tankers from Deep Cove, with the intake utilising the discharge from the tailrace tunnel.

Te Anau's catchment appears to be getting wetter. Hydrological studies point to a steady increase in inflows for the lake, amounting to between 10 and 15 cumecs since 1965. Te Anau's mean outflow is about 275 cumecs – more than half the total for the entire Waiau catchment. In contrast, the Manapouri catchment harvests 127 cumecs, Mararoa (Mavora Lakes) 32 cumecs and Monowai 13 cumecs.

Deep Lakes

Cryptodepression is the term used to describe a freshwater lake whose floor is below the present-day sea level. Thanks to over-deepening of valley floors by glacial advances, several large Fiordland lakes have bottoms that are considerably lower than sea level. The deepest part of Lake Manapouri is 266m below sea level, Te Anau's deepest point is 215m below.

An aquatic earthworm *Diporochaeta aquatica*, endemic to Fiordland, is found at a depth of 100-150m in Lake Manapouri. The same species, which grows to 38mm in length, occurs also at Tunnel Burn and Takahe Valley.

Lakes at a Glance

Lake Te Anau

Area	352 sq km
Catchment	3,095 sq km
Maximum depth	417m
Length (long axis)	60km
Mean height above sea level	202m

Lake Manapouri

Area	142 sq km
Catchment	1,388 sq km
Maximum depth	444m
Length (long axis)	28km
Mean height above sea level	178m

Lake Monowai

Area	32 sq km
Catchment	230 sq km
Maximum depth	161m
Length (long axis)	21km
Mean height above sea level	195m

Right: *Shoreline vegetation at Supply Bay, Lake Manapouri. The jointed rush grades into manuka.*
Neville Peat

Above: Iti lacustris, *a native cress, here in flower, has evolved in the turf zone on the shores of Lakes Manapouri and Te Anau – its only known locations.*

Peter Johnson

On the fringe

No fewer than seven vegetation zones have been identified on the shores of Lakes Manapouri and Te Anau – a reflection of the dynamic nature of the shorelines of these large lakes. A distinct pattern of plant communities has evolved where the lake edge shelves and numerous environmental factors apply, including slope and aspect, beach material (gravel, sand, silt or mud), the impact of winds, rainfall gradient and tolerance to flooding and dry spells.

At the wet (lower) end of the zonation pattern are the aquatic plants, which extend to about 6m below mean water level. They include masses of *Isoetes alpinus* and the feathery bronze or dark-green foliage of water milfoil *Myriophyllum triphyllum* and *M. propinquum*.

Next comes a turf zone where the plants (some 90 herbaceous native species in total) have to cope with periods of submergence and exposure and also wave action. A rare plant in the turf zone is *Iti lacustris*, a cress with tiny white flowers, discovered in 1971 by botanist Peter Johnson in the course of surveys associated with the Manapouri power project. With no close relatives in New Zealand or overseas, it acquired a Maori name (*Iti*, the genus, means small).

The lake-shore turf zone contains two other Fiordland endemics – *Brachyscome linearis* and the buttercup *Ranunculus recens* var *lacustris*. The huge range of shore species includes the

threatened *Hydatella inconspicua*, which was found on the Te Anau, Manapouri and Hauroko lake shores in the early 1990s. A tufted plant, only 2-4cm tall, it was previously known only from dune lakes in Northland. Other threatened species are *Gratiola nana*, *Tetrachondra hamiltonii* and *Deschampsia caespitosa*.

Above the turf is the sedge zone where *Carex gaudichaudiana* forms belts up to 50m wide. This sedge gives way to a zone dominated by the jointed rush or oioi *Leptocarpus similis*. Up to 1m tall, jointed rush adds a soft texture to the lake-shore vegetation that grades into shrubland dominated by manuka *Leptospermum scoparium*. The roots of manuka will tolerate submersion for long periods, but trees will be dwarfed in the wetter sites closest to

Beech defoliation

The trees below are mountain beech on the shores of Lake Te Anau, at Brod Bay. The grey tinge on the trees is defoliation caused periodically by the yellow-green and red caterpillars of *Proteodes carnifex*, the mountain beech moth, a native depressariid.

Outbreaks of defoliation have been recorded in the Te Anau-Manapouri region in 1952-55, 1965-70, 1977-79 and the summer of 1996. No control measures are needed as the trees recover. The dramatic collapse of moth numbers following such an epidemic is caused by natural enemies, including a minute native wasp species and two flies that parasitise the caterpillars. The pinkish, sometimes yellow, adults of *P. carnifex* have a wingspan of about 20mm. Females lay up to 300 eggs singly on the underside of the mountain beech leaves. The larvae feed on the host through winter and spring and into early summer, by which time the damage is highly visible. By mid-January the larva is fully grown and constructs a cocoon of silk-joined leaves to enable it to pupate. Adults emerge to disperse and mate in February.

Although most trees recover, the oldest ones may die from having their crowns weakened. Epidemics fade away after two or three years, underlining the resilience of mountain beech to such events.

Neville Peat

Above: *Mixed beech/podocarp forest beside a wetland close to the Lake Manapouri shoreline at Shallow Bay. The tall spire-like trees are kahikatea* Dacrycarpus dacryioides.
Neville Peat

the water. This gives the lake-shore vegetation a streamlined profile, which provides a measure of protection from wind damage for the taller trees inland. Between the manuka zone and the forest proper, there is commonly a mixed shrub zone.

A prostrate, sprawling native broom grows around the shores of Lakes Manapouri and Te Anau, generally under manuka. It was named *Carmichaelia lacustris* and was considered endemic to these lake shores until recently when a revision synonymised it with the more widespread but still threatened *C. juncea*.

On some sandy shores, trees of kowhai *Sophora microphyllum*, the southern species, have established above flood level at the edge of the forest.

Treasure islands

Lake Manapouri's 33 islands are botanical treasure islands. The vegetation on them is virtually unmodified by introduced browsing animals. On only two islands – the largest ones, Pomona (260ha) and Rona (55ha) – have red deer caused any notice able damage in the past.

Thirty-one islands support trees and shrubs; two small ones have herbs only. The most telling feature of the forest on the wooded islands is its complex understorey.

Untouched by deer or possums, the orchids *Earina autumnalis* and *E. mucronata* (which has longer and narrower leaves) festoon the understorey. Palatable species such as broadleaf *Griselinia littoralis*, southern rata *Metrosideros umbellata*, three-finger *Pseudopanax colensoi* and numerous fern species are allowed to achieve their potential here.

Mountain beech *Nothofagus solandri* var *cliffortioides* forms the canopy on the islands, with silver beech *N. menziesii* making an occasional appearance.

The island flora includes no fewer than eight podocarps, with Hall's totara *Podocarpus hallii* the commonest species. Rimu, kahikatea, matai and miro occur less commonly. Understorey trees and shrubs include 13 *Coprosma* species, mapou *Myrsine australis*, *Olearia arborescens*, kohuhu *Pittosporum tenuifolium* and lancewood (horoeka) *Pseudopanax crassifolius*. On some rocky sites on the islands is a small (1m high) shrub *Gaultheria rupestris*, which is more commonly found west of the main divide. Forty-six fern species are on the list (of 195 species nationwide). Flax and jointed rush are common on the shores.

If Lake Manapouri had been raised 8m for hydro-electric power generation as was proposed in the 1960s, 17 islands would have been submerged and a further seven would have been reduced to wave-washed rocks. The vulnerability of these islands was used as an argument against lake-raising during the Save Manapouri Campaign.

Above: *Mahara Island, Lake Manapouri.*
Neville Peat

Above: *Orchids grow prolifically on the Manapouri islands, including this common species, Easter orchid* Earina autumnalis.
Neville Peat

FISH

Only 12 species of native fish are recorded from the Waiau catchment and Fiordland in general. More species are bound to come to light as surveys are carried out in the remoter streams, rivers and lakes.

The most common native species are long-finned eel *Anguilla dieffenbachii*, red-finned bully *Gobiomorphus huttoni* and four galaxiid species – giant kokopu *Galaxias argenteus*, banded kokopu *G. fasciatus*, inanga *G. maculatus* and koaro *G. brevipinnis*. Their juveniles are better known as whitebait. After spawning in estuaries, usually in autumn, the tiny fry are swept to sea where they remain for about six months. Land-locked populations of koaro, which are adept at negotiating rapids and waterfalls, have been found in high-altitude lakes and tarns. Giant kokopu live at low altitudes, usually in dark streams overhung by forest or flax-lined backwaters. They stay hidden by day, emerging at night to feed.

There are numerous non-migratory galaxiid species in New Zealand. *Galaxias vulgaris*, the common river galaxiid, occurs in the Waiau catchment, including rivers in the Takitimu Mountains and Longwood Range. Little is known about Fiordland's other non-migratory galaxiids.

Red-finned bullies, about 10cm in length, are common in bouldery streams in forest or open areas. As with the migratory galaxiids, the larvae go to sea (spawning is in late winter or spring) and juveniles return when they are about 15mm long.

Long-finned eels are long-distance travellers. As small elvers,

Above: *For much of its journey to Lake Te Anau, the Eglinton River chuckles steadily through a series of grassy flats and tracts of beech forest. It is a rich habitat for fresh-water life, especially aquatic invertebrates.*
Neville Peat

Above: *Giant kokopu* Galaxias argenteus *is the largest of the native galaxiids and one of the most secretive. It may exceed 50cm in length and weigh more than 2.5kg.*
G.A. Eldon

having spawned at sea somewhere in the tropical South Pacific, they enter rivers where they remain until adulthood. Adults migrate to sea and the distant tropics to spawn. Lamprey *Geotria australis*, less conspicuous, also have a marine phase, with juveniles going to sea after spawning and returning as adults. Adults can negotiate low waterfalls and rapids.

Torrentfish *Cheimarrichthys fosteri* inhabit swift-flowing waters in Fiordland. They are at sea as juveniles and enter the rivers in spring. Stokell's smelt *Stokellia anisodon* was described in 1941 by Gerald Stokell from specimens collected at the mouth of the Waiau River by the then director of the Southland Museum, J.H. Sorenson. The small (65-95mm) mainly marine species utilises river estuaries to spawn but strangely has not been re-collected at the Waiau lagoons or in any other river south of the Waitaki since the 1940s.

Only three introduced species, all salmonids, are found in the region – brown trout, released into the Waiau in the 1870s; rainbow trout, released into Lake Te Anau in the 1920s; and Atlantic salmon *Salmo salar*, which were liberated in Te Anau tributaries, chiefly the Upukerora River, in 1908-11. Very few Atlantic salmon remain. Lakes Gunn and Fergus, at the head of the Eglinton Valley, were thought to be harbouring the last of them. The trout have not established large populations in western rivers, possibly because of the flood-prone conditions.

Fiordland may be the last refuge of a native trout-like fish, the grayling *Prototroctes oxyrhynchus*, which disappeared from New Zealand rivers and creeks during the first half of the twentieth century. Known to Maori as upokororo, the grayling grew to about 28cm. It was variably coloured – brown or red, sometimes bluish. The species was recorded inhabiting the Seaforth River, which runs into Dusky Sound, by early conservationist Richard Henry. The grayling was widely distributed throughout the North and South Islands, and common enough in the nineteenth century to be considered a 'fish and chip' species.

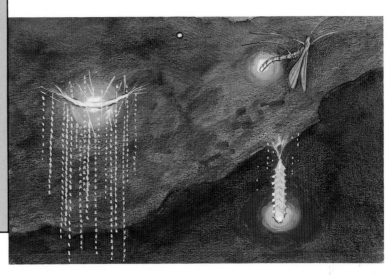

EGLINTON VALLEY

In terms of size and natural features, the Eglinton Valley is the most important valley in the Te Anau catchment. It is also of considerable strategic value. To most people, the Eglinton is a thoroughfare, the only way into or out of Milford Sound by road – fast tarseal. Bus passengers are liable to nod off. For nature lovers, though, the valley is something special.

Relatively low-lying for much of its 40km length, the valley contains a series of broad grassy river flats bordered by beech forest that sweeps upwards towards a treeline in the subalpine zone. Rainfall is plentiful at more than 2,000mm a year.

The grasslands, tawny 'lakes' amid the dark-green backdrop, are dominated by introduced species as a result of a long history of pastoral farming, going back to 1859. Browntop *Agrostis capillaris* predominates, with native sedges occurring in damp hollows and toetoe *Cortaderia richardii* on drier edges. The south end of the valley contains some speargrass *Aciphylla* aff. *glaucescens* but native dry grassland species such as this are otherwise rare.

Three species of beech occur in the Eglinton – mountain, silver and red. Red beech *Nothofagus fusca*, largest of the native beech species, is not common in Fiordland. The extensive stands of it in the Eglinton are testimony to the valley's comparatively mild climate and fertility.

Biologists recognise the valley's highly productive nature, explained at least in part by the extent of forest edges, both along the river flats and in the subalpine zone. Because insect populations are abundant, insectivorous birds do well here. So do bats. The edges of wetlands are also biologically rich.

The valley has significant populations of threatened species such as yellowhead, yellow-crowned parakeet, South Island kaka and long-tailed bat. Flocks of kaka are common in the valley in February-March. They are late autumn breeders.

For forest birds in general, the Eglinton is prime habitat. It is a stronghold for South Island robin and South Island rifleman. New Zealand falcons are conspicuous. Paradise shelducks inhabit the flats, and black-billed gulls breed in colonies on the river gravel.

Opposite: Small bogs, typically oval-shaped, occur in the Upper Eglinton beech forest – oases for native heaths, herbs, cushions and mosses. The flattened, trailing foliage of the sub-shrub Dracophyllum prostratum *is eye-catching. The taller* D. oliveri *is also present. Wire rush* Empodisma minus *is widespread, giving way to moss* Sphagnum cristatum *in the wetter areas. The sundews* Drosera arcturi *and* D. spathulata *are common. At the margins of the bog are the shrubs* Olearia bullata, *a small-leaved black-stemmed tree daisy, and mountain toatoa (celery pine)* Phyllocladus alpinus, *whose blue-green foliage is highly aromatic (pine smell). The genus name refers to the flattened leaf-like branches or cladodes. Red pollen is distinctive on male trees in December.*
Neville Peat

Below: *Bog vegetation fancy-work, Upper Eglinton: a mat of yellow-orange moss* Sphagnum cristatum *is laced with glaucous* Dracophyllum prostratum, *framed by* Androstoma empetrifolia, *and scatter-stitched with wire rush* Empodisma minus.
Neville Peat

Right: *Mohua.*
Ian Southey

Icon songster

Pretty to look at, delightful to listen to, the yellowhead *Mohoua ochrocephala* is at home in the Eglinton forest, where nest sites (holes in old beech trees) and food resources are plentiful.

Known to Maori as mohua (which name is echoed in its genus name) and to early Europeans as bush canary on account of its beautiful trilling song and bright yellow head and breast, the yellowhead is found only in the South Island. Populations (extended families) occur in many forested valleys of Fiordland, but the Eglinton population is of particular interest because it has been the subject of an intensive study since 1990.

Yellowheads are often seen moving through the canopy in family groups, foraging as they go, sometimes in the company of yellow-crowned parakeets. Staple elements of their diet are moths, caterpillars, beetles, beetle larvae, bugs, weta and spiders. Their habit of scrambling up and down tree trunks can reduce the tips of their tail feathers to spiny shafts.

The nest is usually high above the ground in a hole in a rotten trunk. Yellowheads prefer small entrances that open into a chamber. Eggs are laid – usually two to four – in October-November, with the female doing all the incubating. Her mate and 'helpers' within the extended family will take turns to feed her. Other females may assist with the incubation.

Yellowhead populations everywhere have declined markedly through the twentieth century because of predation, by stoats in particular. Incubating females are especially vulnerable to attack from stoats. In yellowhead strongholds such as the Eglinton Valley, the Department of Conservation has instituted stoat control measures (trapping and poisoning). By the mid-1990s, the programme appeared to be having an effect. In four years, the yellowheads in the Eglinton study area had increased from four pairs to 25.

The yellowhead has become an icon among forest birds because of its attractive appearance and song, and its threatened status. Related species are brown creeper or pipipi *Mohoua novaeseelandiae*, a South Island/Stewart Island-only species, and whitehead or popokatea *Mohoua albicilla*, which is found only in the North Island.

'Mast' seasons

When beech trees seed en masse every three to seven years, the event is called a 'mast' season. Insects become abundant, mice populations explode and bird species also do well. There are rich pickings for stoats, *Mustela erminea*, which find nesting yellowheads especially easy prey.

Of the three mustelid species introduced into New Zealand (ferret, stoat and weasel), the stoat is by far the most dangerous for forest birds. But it is a marked mustelid in the Eglinton Valley. Long-term stoat studies in the Eglinton show that home ranges are usually about 200ha but may be as large as 800ha. Male stoats, a third larger than females, have the larger home ranges. But stoats may also migrate long distances. One radio-tagged female travelled 65km in under a month (it was trapped at Burwood Bush).

Long-tailed bat – A high-revving motor

Bats are New Zealand's only indigenous land mammals. The long-tailed bat or pekapeka *Chalinolobus tuberculatus* is common in the Eglinton Valley where the population is estimated at 1,000.

With a body the size of a mouse and a wingspan of 25-28cm, long-tailed bats are sometimes mistaken for swallows or fantails when they fly at or after dusk. Body weights are 10-11g for females and about 9g for males. Females routinely fly with their babies, which are comparatively large. Some even stay attached to a nipple in flight. Astonishingly, one female was found commuting with an 8g youngster.

Studies carried out since 1990 have shown the Eglinton bats feed for two to four hours after the onset of darkness. They then rest through the rest of the night and resume feeding at dawn. Insectivorous, they eat *Stenoperla* stoners, dobsonflies, *Aoraia* moths, black flies and mosquitoes.

Miniature radio transmitters attached to selected bats in the Eglinton Valley have allowed scientists to track movements. Bats can fly as fast as 60kph but more usually 30kph. One female travelled 21km in a single flight. Journeys of 40 to 100km a night are not uncommon. Home ranges can be as large as 90 sq km. This little bat is like a high-revving motor. A frenetic feeder, it can put on 3g in body-weight after a night's foraging. But long-tailed bats also require extended rest periods. In colder weather they develop a state of torpor, during which their metabolic rate slows considerably. It is thought this could enhance longevity. Small bats overseas are known to live to about 35 years.

Adults raise one young per year, and they tend to begin breeding between two and three years of age. A typical nest is located in a hole in a red beech tree about 20m above the ground. Holes or notches are also used for roosting. About a third of all roosts in the Eglinton are in standing dead trees.

New Zealand's bats

One unusual finding of the studies of bats has been the habit of long-tailed bats to change roosts reasonably often. The reasons for this are unclear. By changing home roosts they may be trying to deceive predators such as moreporks. The tactic may also be in the interests of hygiene – avoiding parasite build-ups.

New Zelanad has three described native bat species in two genera, *Chalinolobus* and *Mystacina*.

C. tuberculatus, the long-tailed bat, is widely distributed. Most large tracts of native forest will have resident populations. Of the two short-tailed bats, *Mystacina robusta* is probably extinct and there are three allopatric subspecies of the rare lesser short-tailed bat, *M. tuberculata*, making five bat taxa in total.

Left: *A male long-tailed bat, Eglinton Valley.*
Rod Morris

WETLANDS Modest mosaics

A wallowing place of long-gone glaciers and a receptacle of outwash gravels, the Te Anau Basin east of Lakes Te Anau and Manapouri contains depressions and areas of limited drainage in which wetlands have developed.

Within the basin, there are at least seven significant and distinct wetlands, the most notable being Kepler Mire, Dome Mire and Dismal Swamp.

The altitude in the basin ranges from 180m to 360m. Rainfall averages 1,100mm a year. Frosts are frequent in winter, and fog may persist for a day or two in lower-lying areas.

Differences in drainage, the water table, the extent of ponded water and soil fertility account for variations in the character of the wetlands. Because of the underlying peat, mire conditions predominate in most areas. Little visited or admired except by wetland enthusiasts and scientists, the wetlands represent ecosystems that are largely undisturbed and rich in species.

Pollens, spores and micro-fossils buried in the peat have helped scientists map the vegetation history of the area.

Within each wetland is a mosaic of plant life, although the larger the wetland the more varied the vegetation. More than 200 plant species have been recorded from the wetlands and associated margins, providing habitat for native birds, fish and invertebrate fauna, some of which are threatened or uncommon.

The plant communities vary. Infertile peatlands feature wire rush *Empodisma minus,* which forms wiry green and brown carpets overlying tangled spongy masses of white and pink roots. Bog pine *Halocarpus bidwillii* and turpentine shrub *Dracophyllum oliveri* are also common in this community. On more fertile areas the *Carex* sedges appear, including the grass-like sward-forming *C. gaudichaudiana, C. diandra, C. sinclairii* and the impressive tussocks of *C. secta* or purei, which can reach 3m tall. *Sphagnum* mosses (bright-green *S. falcatulum* and yellow-green *S. cristatum*) and the sedges *Baumea rubiginosa* and *B. tenax* may surround pools and fill wet hollows. Tussock grasslands feature copper tussock *Chionochloa rubra* ssp *cuprea.* Manuka *Leptospermum scoparium* is the commonest shrub on the edges, where it forms dense stands.

The most conspicuous birds are in the family *Anatidae* (swans, geese and ducks), including paradise shelduck, Canada goose, New Zealand shoveler, grey teal, grey duck, mallard and New Zealand scaup. Two shags are frequently seen, although not in number – black shag *Phalacrocorax carbo* and little shag *P. melanoleucos.* The herons are well represented in the form of Australasian bittern, white-faced heron, white heron and cattle egret. The bittern or matuku *Botaurus poiciloptilus* keeps itself well camouflaged in dense vegetation and is more often heard

Invertebrate life

The sedge, herb and shrub communities associated with wetlands are home to a large variety of invertebrate species.

Most noteworthy in the drier areas are the spiders, flies and grass moths, which fly up when disturbed by day.

Among the moths there is a southern element, represented by the elegantly patterned *Orocrambus thymiastes* and the larger *Heloxycanus patricki.* The latter's larvae feed on *Sphagnum* from inside deep tunnels, which are often below the water table. Like a lot of mire fauna, adults emerge late in the season when the wetlands are at their driest.

Open water is home to two damselflies – the common blue *Austrolestes colensonis* and redcoat *Xanthocnemis zealandica* – and the larger dragonfly *Procordulia smithii,* which has a 50mm wingspan. All three species, in the order *Odonata,* have aquatic carnivorous larvae that take up to four years to develop into adulthood.

On hot summer days adults of *P. smithii* will patrol over a pond surface looking out for a mate. Males set up territories along a stretch of waterside vegetation. They will see off other males and attempt to mate with any female that enters their territory.

Similarly, redcoat and blue damselflies also defend areas. In addition, redcoat males are often seen swarming around an eligible female.

All three species are predacious both as larvae and as adults, feeding on smaller invertebrates. As larvae, they in turn are fed on by larger larvae or adults, such as water beetle larvae and other *Odonata* larvae, while the adults are taken by spiders, wasps and birds.

Above: *The dragonfly* Uropetala carovei *(length up to 86mm) is common around the wetlands of Fiordland. New Zealand has two species of giant dragonfly of this genus.* U. carovei *lives in the North Island and western parts of the South Island, and the similar-looking* U. chiltoni, *is found only in eastern South Island. Their long-lived larvae live in tunnels in seepages and streambanks and prey on smaller animals.*

Wynston Cooper

(the males have a booming call) than seen. The white-faced heron *Ardea novaehollandiae* is a relative newcomer, blown in from Australia, with breeding confirmed in southern New Zealand in the 1940s. The cattle egret *Bubulcus ibis coromandus* is an even more recent arrival. Originally from Asia, more recently Australia, cattle egrets began showing up in New Zealand in numbers in the 1960s. Migrants to New Zealand winter here.

The Australasian harrier *Circus approximans*, distinguished by its gliding flight, commonly patrols the wetlands in search of food. The South Island fernbird *Bowdleria punctata,* on the other hand, makes only short fluttering flights across the wetland vegetation. The rails are less obvious, being poorly flighted or little inclined to fly. Pukeko *Porphyrio melanotus*, belonging to the same genus as takahe, is the commonest rail, socialising in family groups in the open. Marsh crake also live in the Te Anau Basin wetlands, but this bird is secretive and is rarely seen. With many wetlands in other parts of the country destroyed by agricultural and other development, the Te Anau Basin wetlands take on added importance as refuges for threatened wetland birds.

To the south, at the northern edge of the Waiau Basin, another important wetland occurs – the Borland Mire. Located near the mouth of the Borland Valley, it is an example, now rare in New Zealand, of a raised bog. Bog pine is a feature shrub. The small rosette herb *Oreostylidium subulatum*, occupying a genus of its own, endemic to New Zealand, is found here. Another notable plant, found around the edge of the mire, is the daisy *Celmisia glandulosa*, which has distinctive toothed dark-green leaves.

Te Waewae lagoons

What used to be New Zealand's second largest river, the Waiau, greets the sea not with an estuary but with a series of long narrow lagoons trapped behind extensive gravel dunes. These lagoons at Te Waewae Bay are a significant natural feature, providing habitat for many species of native fish and birds. With the reduction in flows as a result of the Manapouri power scheme, there were major changes in the structure and hydrology of the lagoons and a subsequent loss of natural habitat. A restoration project in the mid-1990s aims to give the lagoons a new lease of life.

Although the largest and most important wetlands lie outside (east of) Fiordland National Park, there are a few which do enjoy national park status. They include the Garnock Burn, Monument Mire and Amoebid Mires. The Amoebid Mire, between the upper Waiau River and Shallow Bay, is notable for its cushion plants – comb sedge *Oreobolus pectinatus*, which forms dense hard cushions, and the moss-like *Centrolepis ciliata*. Occasionally the *Oreobolus* cushions are colonised by bladderwort *Utricularia monanthos*, which has small purplish flowers.

In the Te Anau Basin most of the significant wetlands are protected and under the control of the Department of Conservation. Forest or shrubland once surrounded them; most of it is now cleared for farming.

The role of wetlands in flood control and the maintenance of water quality is now recognised. Wetlands also provide an important link in food chains.

A mire is a type of wetland found usually on peaty areas, poor in nutrients (oligotrophic) and fed by rainwater rather than rivers or streams. Swamps, on the other hand, are nutrient-rich, and water flows more freely. Plant life in a mire is characteristically slow growing. Shrubs are often stunted. Dome mires have a raised central area.

Above: *Kepler Mire string bogs. The elongated ponds are aligned at right angles to a gentle slope running towards Home Creek. The Takitimu Mountains are in the distance.*
Chris Rance

Right: *Where the boggy ground gives way to a drier footing at the northern margins of the Kepler Mire, a wide range of plant species is to be found. The shrubs include bog pine* Halocarpus bidwillii, Coprosma cuneata, Corokia cotoneaster, *matagouri* Discaria toumatou, Cassinia vauvilliersii *and numerous heath-like shrubs, including* Androstoma empetrifolia, Gaultheria depressa *and* G. macrostigma. *Among the herbs are* Astelia nervosa, Hypericum *sp and* Celmisia *aff* gracilenta. *The monocots include silver tussock, blue tussock and* Carpha alpina. *This sort of margin attracts an array of insects – grasshoppers, craneflies, dragonflies, tussock butterflies and numerous moth species.*
Neville Peat

Dome Mire/Dismal Swamp

About 10km north-east of Te Anau township is the 500ha Dome Mire and Dismal Swamp. At 250-270m above sea level, the complex is slightly higher than the Kepler Mire.

The northern portion is a raised (3m high) dome dotted with pools. The infertile, rain-fed peatland is dominated by wire rush. In the centre of the area is Lake Te Aroha and a large stand of manuka. To the south is Dismal Swamp, reflecting a higher water table. The swamp's fertility is reflected in the presence of various sedges in the genera *Carex* and *Baumea*.

Of interest is the presence of silver pine *Lagarostrobus colensoi* – the only known site east of the main divide for this podocarp, which has been logged extensively on the West Coast in the past. Its tolerance of boggy ground made it a target for fence posts.

The wetland's plant list of over 100 species contains two uncommon plants, the small orchid *Acianthus fornicatus* and the moss *Acrocladium cuspidatum*.

Kepler Mire

The Kepler Mire east of Lake Manapouri, covering more than 900ha (altitude 220-230m), is the largest wetland in the Te Anau Basin complex. Its dome is about 3m higher at the centre than at the margins.

The peat development here is impressive, reaching depths of up to 4.7m. The total volume of peat in this one mire is estimated at 20.5 million cubic metres. Filling old channels of the Waiau River and forming lobes in a glacial depression adjacent to low moraine hills, the Kepler Mire contains an outstanding string-bog complex, the main feature of its southern portion.

The string-bog is made up of numerous split-level ponds and narrow pools arranged in a 'staircase'. After heavy rain the pools overflow, each spilling water to an adjacent lower one. Home Creek provides drainage south to the lower Waiau arm of Lake Manapouri.

More than 100 plant species have been recorded in the Kepler Mire. Wire rush, turpentine shrub and tangle fern *Gleichenia dicarpa* generally dominate areas lying above the water table. Notable among the shrubs are yellow-silver pine *Lepidothamnus intermedius* and pygmy pine *L. laxifolius*. The latter, perhaps the world's smallest conifer, reaching no more than half a metre in height, has wiry yellow-green or glaucous foliage and a sprawling habit.

Aquatic plants include the endemic mud pondweed or rerewai *Potamogeton suboblongus*, whose leathery bright-green leaves float on the surface. The Kepler Mire is also valued for its mosses, including two species which are uncommon locally or nationally – *Eucamptodon inflatus* and *Campylopus kirkii*.

The Gorge

The Gorge, on the eastern edge of the Te Anau Basin, is a tussock wilderness. Large tracts of eastern Fiordland must have looked like this before farming came along. Beech forest (Burwood Bush) provides a dark-green fringe beyond the brilliantly hued copper tussock *Chionochloa rubra* ssp *cuprea*, which cloaks the low saddle dividing the Waiau catchment from the Oreti on the road between Te Anau and Lumsden.

Among the invertebrate fauna, moths are especially abundant in The Gorge area. Of the 2,000-plus moth species so far recorded in New Zealand, several hundred inhabit The Gorge's grasslands, shrublands and herbfield areas. Over half of these are active by day (diurnal), sporting bright and contrasting colours (typically yellow/black and orange/blue-grey).

The noctuid moth *Meterana meyricci* (wingspan 40mm) has spectacular colouration – dark green and white forewings hiding bright pink and grey hindwings. Its larvae feed on the foliage of the low shrub *Pimelea oreophila*. Perhaps the adult colours result from chemicals in the food plant, ingested by the larvae.

Other conspicuous moths found in The Gorge are the giant *Aoraia dinodes* (wingspan 65mm), tiger moth *Metacrias strategica* and colourful diurnal geometrids *Asaphodes cinnabari* and *Dasyuris transaurea*.

Above: *Extensive grasslands of copper tussock* Chionochloa rubra cuprea *are eye-catching in The Gorge. Associated shrublands feature the small-leaved tree daisy* Olearia bullata *and spiny matagouri* Discaria toumatou.
Neville Peat

Rising above the copper tussock in The Gorge are flowerheads of the speargrass Aciphylla aff glaucescens. *This crowning cluster of flowerheads is well over 2m tall.*
Neville Peat

The Wilderness

One of the most unusual and intriguing habitats in the Waiau catchment is a patch of shrubland about 20km south-east of Te Anau that is dominated by bog pine *Halocarpus bidwillii*.

People driving the Lumsden-Te Anau road (State Highway 94) pass through the middle this habitat, which is known as The Wilderness Scientific Reserve. It is a frost flat, lying close to the Mararoa River.

The 88ha reserve, contrasting sharply with the surrounding farmland, gives a glimpse of what the general area might have looked like before agriculture transformed it with fenced pasture and exotic trees and hedgerows. Bog pine shrubs up to 4m tall are spread throughout the reserve in a loose shrubby woodland. Other shrub species found here include *Leonohebe odora*, *Corokia cotoneaster*, *Cassinia vauvilliersii*, *Dracophyllum uniflorum*, manuka *Leptospermum scoparium* and shrubs of the *Coprosma parviflora* group.

A dense ground cover of mosses, liverworts and lichens keeps the shrubby 'islands' spaced and, with the native heath plants and herbs, generally contributes to the open character of the site. Among the heaths and prostrate shrubs are patotara *Leucopogon fraseri*, *L. colensoi*, snowberry *Gaultheria depressa*, *Coprosma petriei*, *Coriaria sarmentosa* and *Pimelea prostrata*. Herbs include a native ground-hugging lily *Herpolirion novae-zelandiae*, which has blue-white flowers and glaucous grass-like leaves. Among exotic plant pests posing threats here are European broom and heather. Rabbits are also a threat.

Special insects

The black cricket *Pteronemobius bigelowi*, common in open areas, is found in The Wilderness Reserve. Moth species include *Scythris nigra*, whose food plant is *Leonohebe odora*, and a noctuid moth not recollected in southern New Zealand since 1945 – *Aletia argentaria* (wingspan 33mm). The name alludes to its silver colour. The Wilderness is the type locality for the species. For the most part the insect fauna is typical of open areas.

Below: *Bogpine* Halocarpus bidwillii *is the dominant shrub at The Wilderness Scientific Reserve. Moss carpets the ground.*
Brian Patrick

THE NORTH
High and mighty

The North is the Fiordland most people identify with. It contains such icons as the Milford Track, Sutherland Falls, Mitre Peak, Mt Tutoko, Milford Sound, Eglinton Valley, Hollyford Valley and Homer Tunnel. The North is the more accessible half of the region, because of the Milford Road.

This chapter is concerned with the terrestrial north, from the Kepler Mountains north to Big Bay, which is where South Westland begins. The mountains are higher in the north than in the south – higher and sharper. Their height accentuates their steepness. Here the Southern Alps and the main divide lose their separate identities. The topography becomes a criss-crossing jumble of valleys and mountain ranges in which it is difficult to perceive a pattern.

The Darran Mountains, projecting Fiordland's highest peaks, form the southernmost high-alpine range in New Zealand. Their north-south alignment sets them at an oblique angle to the Southern Alps. If you can imagine the Alps as a exclamation mark, the Darrans form the full-stop, their peaks punctuating the sky! The highest of them are Mt Tutoko (2,746m), which overlooks Milford Sound one way and the Hollyford Valley the other, nearby Mt Madeline (2,537m), and Mt Christina (2,502m) which dominates the skyline above The Divide. The Darrans are high enough to retain permanent ice and snowfields, and a few glaciers of modest size.

In the north the Darrans lose their stature rather abruptly. They have been uplifted along the line of the Alpine Fault, which separates the crystalline gneiss and diorite of the Darrans from the much older greywacke of the land to the west, epitomised by the low forested hills of the John O'Groats River catchment.

Mt Pembroke is in this area – a dramatic example of uplift in the landscape. Within just 5km of open ocean, this mountain rises to a height of 2,000m. Nearby, the Alpine Fault leaves the land at Stripe Point.

To the south a series of mountain ranges divides the three fiords of Lake Te Anau. North to south, they are the Franklin, Stuart, Murchison and Kepler Mountains. The first two are named after nineteenth century international explorers, the last two honour overseas scientists – Murchison, a British geologist, and Kepler, a German astronomer.

Much about the flora and fauna of the North is unique, rare and special – the alpine elements, in particular, which comprise the main focus of this chapter.

Plant species endemic to Fiordland are surprisingly numerous, although the fact that the majority are found in the alpine zone is perhaps less surprising when one realises that somewhat

Above: *The mountainous north – Lady of the Snows (1,832m) and cirque lake, above Poison Bay, south of Milford Sound.*
Tony Lilleby /DOC

Right: *Catseye Bay, between Bligh and George Sounds, displays the typical U-form of northern valleys and fiords. It has a well-developed dune system that supports a diversity of dune plants. The prominent orange plant on the dunes is the sedge Pingao. Back in the forest, some of the rata trees are in full bloom. This bay, being exposed to the ocean current flowing south down the South Westland coast, is at risk of infestation by weeds such as broom, gorse and marram.*
Chris Rance

more than half of all native plant species in New Zealand are alpine. It is estimated that 8 per cent of our alpine plant species are found only in Fiordland or in the western Otago mountains just to the north. Fiordland's North region is rich in endemics. Among the genera, the speargrasses (*Aciphylla*) are a feature.

Bird life above the treeline is understandably not prolific, but what life exists is of compelling interest. Rock wren and kea are the outstanding species. New Zealand falcon, swiftest bird of all in the mountains, makes forays into the alpine zone in pursuit of live prey. Some forest birds also extend their range into the alpine shrublands and herbfields – bellbird (makomako), grey warbler (riroriro), South Island rifleman (titipounamu), silvereye (tauhou) and South Island tomtit (ngiru-ngiru). Takahe, the flightless, fabled and now endangered Notornis, has a limited distribution. Among the introduced birds, chaffinch is common and widespread above the treeline.

Invertebrate fauna make up for the thinly spread birds. Insect life is diverse and, considering the often cold and wet conditions, remarkably prominent, at least in the warmer months.

Above: *Takahe Valley and Lake Orbell above Lake Te Anau in the Murchison Mountains – takahe country.*
Brian Rance

Left: *Impounded Lake McKenzie is the result of a rock avalanche in the tussock grasslands of the Murchison Mountains.*
Brian Patrick

Avalanches

Avalanches – snow, rock or tree – are common in the North, but especially so in the Darran Mountains. Attracting most attention are the snow avalanches that affect the Milford Road in the Hollyford and Cleddau Valleys between May and November.

More than 40 avalanche paths have been mapped along a 28km stretch of the highway on either side of the Homer Tunnel, starting near the turnoff to the Lower Hollyford and ending about 3km from Milford Sound village. Most of the dangerous paths occur along the last 5km of the highway on the east

Right: *Yet another avalanche on the Milford Road.*
Lou Sanson

Below: *The Upper Hollyford Valley is a rich place for alpine plants and invertebrates, despite being avalanche-prone.*
Neville Peat

side of the Homer Tunnel, where an annual avalanche control programme (aerial bombing) minimises the danger to traffic.

Snow avalanches are usually high-speed events in such steep terrain and are highly destructive, due to the associated windblast. Winds can reach 300kph in front of a snow avalanche, a force sufficient to flatten a mature beech forest.

The vegetation-clearing impact of avalanches, both natural and triggered by the control programme, is clearly evident in the Upper Hollyford above Monkey Creek, where the beech forest suddenly becomes sparse on the lower slopes. In the steepest places, only grasses and a few herbs manage to survive the onslaught of avalanches, finding root on narrow ledges.

Tree avalanches occur when, usually after heavy rain, roots give way in the thin soils and a section of forest plummets to the valley floor. The landscape is striped with them, most noticeably the steep slopes around Lakes Te Anau and Manapouri. Rock avalanches are less common because of the solid nature of the mountains, and they are generally less destructive.

Treeline

The treeline is the upper limit at which forest – in Fiordland's case, beech forest – will form, and it is usually governed by summer temperatures.

In northern Fiordland, the treeline generally occurs at about 1,000m above sea level, but it is closer to 900m in valley heads because of colder conditions and the impact of avalanches. In the South, the treeline descends to about 850m, which compares with the 1550m level achieved by beech in central Nelson and the central North Island (Mt Ruapehu).

Two species of beech form the bulk of the forest canopy to the treeline – Silver beech *Nothofagus menziesii* and mountain beech *Nothofagus solandri* var. *cliffortioides*. Shrubs commonly found at the treeline include *Pseudopanax lineare*, *Pittosporum crassicaule*, *Carmichaelia arborea* and *Dracophyllum fiordense*, with the bush lilies *Astelia nervosa* and *A. nivicola* also present.

Silver beech or tawhai grows to about 25m in height in favourable locations, with the trunk reaching 2m across. It tolerates wet conditions, which means it dominates the forest in western areas of Fiordland and forms the treeline virtually throughout. Towards the treeline, however, as the going gets tougher for trees, the silver beech become stunted, little more than 6m tall. Here, in the wet and cloudy conditions, the trees are profusely decorated with lichens, liverworts and mosses – 'goblin forest'.

Mountain beech, on the other hand, has a preference for drier conditions and is more common inland, to the east. It is a smaller tree, reaching about 15m.

Above: *Spectacular Martins Bay. The lower Hollyford River drains Lake McKerrow, an old fiord. Fiordland's tallest peak, Mt Tutoko (2,746m) dominates the skyline at the northern end of the Darran Mountains.*
Brian Rance

Opposite top: *Beech forest creates a remarkably even treeline in the longer valleys. The unusually low treeline limits in Fiordland are explained by the cooler weather of southern latitudes and the cooling effect of the neighbouring ocean. This is Takahe Valley in the Murchison Mountains.*
Peter Johnson

Opposite bottom: *The tropical-looking* Dracophyllum fiordense *lives near the treeline.*
Peter Johnson

MARTINS BAY AND BIG BAY

At the northern boundary of Fiordland are Martins Bay and Big Bay, which boast the longest sandy beaches in Fiordland (6km and 5km respectively) and the most extensive dunes systems. The two bays front a superb, little-modified sequence of habitats, from estuary and lagoon through dunelands to a mosaic of wetlands and mature lowland podocarp forest.

The Hollyford River, having passed through Lake McKerrow, has its mouth at the northern end of Martins Bay. A long sand beach, with dunes 6-8m high, protects McKenzie Lagoon, which is an important habitat for birds such as New Zealand scaup, Australasian bittern and black swan.

A rocky headland (Long Reef), harbouring fur seal and Fiordland crested penguin colonies, separates Martins Bay from Big Bay to the north. The beach is wide and gently-sloping (and frequently used by light aircraft). Driven by the prevailing south-westerly winds, the sand has built up at the northern end of the bay where the dunes reach about 12m in height.

The system of parallel dunes at Big Bay is an outstanding natural feature, especially as the dunes retain much of their native cover: the sand sedge pingao *Desmoschoenus spiralis* and *Poa* grasses, with flax and *Coprosma* shrubs in the hollows. About 1km inland from the beach is forest-clad Waiuna Lagoon, an important breeding area for native waterfowl. Giant kokopu *Galaxias argenteus*, largest of the native galaxiid fish, have been recorded here. The lagoon is drained by the Awarua River, which meanders through old raised beaches to reach the sea at the north end of Big Bay.

Big Bay lies outside Fiordland National Park, but its natural qualities are recognised by its inclusion in the Te Waahipounamu Southwest New Zealand World Heritage Area.

Consistent with the role of the two bays as a geographical boundary, several plants have their northern or southern limits here. Common along the coasts of Fiordland and Stewart Island, muttonbird shrub *Brachyglottis rotundifolia* reaches its northern limit at Martins Bay. Big Bay is the northern limit of the carrot-family herb *Anisotome lyallii* and the southern limit of ngaio *Myoporum laetum*, a medium-sized coastal tree, which is uncommon on the West Coast south of Greymouth.

The bays provide a refuge for a few vulnerable plant species, including the sand milkweed *Euphorbia glauca*, a herb with blue-green leaves and milky juice, and the now uncommon grass *Austrofestuca littoralis*.

Inland, there is an impressive stand of lowland forest, featuring the large podocarps rimu and kahikatea. The understorey is a tangle of vines, climbers, ferns and smaller trees – a jungle compared to the relatively open beech forests higher up. Flowering trees such as kamahi are mixed with the podocarps, and an occasional beech. This is ideal habitat for South Island kaka, which live here in significant numbers. New Zealand pigeon and South Island fernbird are also abundant.

> **The forest inland from Martins and Big Bays is the southernmost major stand of podocarps on the West Coast. It is still intact because no roads have been built through it.**

Important dune species
Austrofestuca littoralis/sand tussock
Calystegia soldanella/sand convolvulus
Carex pumila
Coprosma acerosa/sand coprosma
Desmoschoenus spiralis/pingao
Euphorbia glauca/sand spurge
Geranium sessiliflorum var *arenarium*/shore geranium
Hydrocotyle novaezelandiae
Isolepis nodosa/knobby clubrush
Lagenifera pumila
Myosotis pygmaea var *drucei*/forget-me-not
Pimelea lyallii/sand daphne
Pimelea prostrata
Ranunculus acaulis/buttercup
Scleranthus uniflorus/cushion chickweed
Wahlenbergia congesta/harebell

Wahlenbergia congesta *in flower amongst the dune sedge pingao.*
Chris Rance

Floral heights: Ranunculus serico-phyllus displaying its bright buttercups above Gertrude Saddle at about 1,500m above sea level. Milford Sound is in the distance.
Neville Peat

Above: Dolichoglottis scorzoneroides *at Monkey Creek in the Upper Hollyford.*
Rory Logan

ALPINE PLANTS Masters of adaptation

Despite the rigours of the climate, limited soil development and burial under snow for months on end, the alpine zone harbours a vast array of interesting native plants.

Two herbs exemplify the ability of alpine plants to adapt to the conditions and make the most of their opportunities to grow and reproduce. As the annual melt releases them from under the snow at altitudes above 1,000m, the eyebright *Ourisia caespitosa* and the marsh marigold *Psychrophila (Caltha) obtusa* launch into flower. The *Psychrophila*, a snowbank specialist whose genus name means 'cold-loving', anticipates the moment by developing buds during autumn. By winter the flower is fully formed in the bud, but flowering is suspended over winter. When they do appear, the flowers are white and sweetly scented. The *Ourisia*, with its distinctive notched leaves, produces white flowers with yellow centres and is widely distributed through the North's alpine zone. It can live in wet peaty soils or on rock ledges.

Fiordland's North region is an *Ourisia* grand central station. It accounts for 12 of the 17 taxa in New Zealand – the largest concentration to be found anywhere. South America has some 20 taxa in total, Tasmania one. Among the Fiordland species are *Ourisia remotifolia*, which is found on the main divide from Fiordland to Mt Cook, *O. macrocarpa*, which is confined to Fiordland and western Otago, and *O. crosbyi*, which occurs only in Fiordland and the Longwood Range,

Some alpine species have long flowering seasons (for example, *Leucogenes grandiceps* or South Island edelweiss, and *Forstera sedifolia*), and some carry fruit for months (notably *Coprosma*, *Gaultheria* and *Myrsine* species). Then there are some alpine plants that do not flower every year – *Chionochloa* snow grasses and some speargrasses (*Aciphylla*), for example.

Short flowering seasons are the norm. Perhaps the best-known flowers of the alpine zone, certainly the most showy, are those of the great mountain buttercup *Ranunculus lyallii*, often wrongly called a lily, which flowers over several weeks in November/December. By January, its season is mostly over, but starting to show up about then are the flowers of two common daisies, *Dolichoglottis lyallii* (yellow) and the broader-leaved *D. scorzoneroides* (white). The species hybridise and the results are flowers of lemon or pale apricot shades.

The Homer area is the type locality for a small and little-known alpine daisy, *Abrotanella rostrata*, formally named in mid-1996. Inhabiting fellfield, this daisy grows to only 50mm tall. Its only known sites are in Fiordland and Mount Aspiring National Parks.

The alpine zone contains a number of habitats, each with its own plant community. A shrubland belt, featuring mountain toatoa *Phyllocladus alpinus*, may border the treeline, with the shrubs grading into a zone of tussock grasslands and herbfields. Stream banks, seepages and saturated peaty soils attract their own plants, as do the avalanche chutes, boulderfields, scree slopes and rocky crevices. The nival zone, the most trying place of all for plant growth, appeals only to species that can tolerate extreme cold, persistent snow and a rocky footing.

Speargrass showcase

Fiordland is a showcase area for the group of plants known as speargrasses or spaniards, which belong to the genus *Aciphylla* ('sharp-leaved'). They range from massive tussocks with flowerheads 3m tall (*A. scott-thomsonii*) to low-lying cushions. Their stiff leaves are typically needle-tipped, and the flowerheads on the conspicuous species also carry sharp spines, making them hazardous to trampers and climbers. The growth form of the speargrasses enables them to compete successfully for room among dense grasslands which can overwhelm less robust herbs.

Twelve species occur in Fiordland of a total of 38 (all are found in New Zealand except for two species that occur in Australian mountains). Two species are endemic to Fiordland. *A. leighii* occurs in the Darran Mountains – a diminutive blunt-tipped species, restricted to high-alpine rock crevices above about 1,800m and difficult to find. It is probably confined to just one or two mountains. The second endemic species is *A. takahea*, named after Takahe Valley in the Murchison Mountains, its type locality – a medium-sized dark-green speargrass found in damp sites amid snow tussock, shrubs and herbs and confined to central Fiordland.

Above: *South Island edelweiss Leuco-genes grandiceps, whose flowers and leaves are well adapted to withstand the rigours of the alpine climate.*
Dave Crouchley

Below: Aciphylla leighii *is among the smallest of the speargrasses and one of the most difficult to locate, seemingly restricted to the high-alpine zone of the Darran Mountains. In rosettes about 70mm wide, it forms patches of up to 2m in diameter. The blunt leaves are only 50mm long. Discovered in the 1930s, it has been collected only three times, most recently in 1994 at an altitude of 1,830m on Mt Syme.*
Brian Rance

Fiordland *Aciphylla* species (with distribution elsewhere noted)

A. congesta (western Otago, South Westland)
A. crenulata (main divide)
A. crosby-smithii (Fiordland, western Otago)
A. divisa (main divide)
A. horrida (main divide)
A. leighii (Darran Mountains only)
A. lyallii (main divide)
A. multisecta (main divide)
A. pinnatifida (east to Umbrella Mountains)
A. scott-thomsonii (southern South Island)
A. spedenii (east to Eyre Mountains)
A. takahea (central Fiordland only)

Above: *Wilting slightly on a warm afternoon in the Gertrude Valley are the flowers and leaves of* Hoheria lyallii.
Neville Peat

Right: *Gertrude Valley, looking towards its junction with the Upper Hollyford.*
Neville Peat

Above: *A common grass on the valley floor is the small fine-leaved* Rytidosperma setifolium, *which produces tightly bunched seedheads in late summer.*
Neville Peat

A WALK IN THE GERTRUDE

The Gertrude Valley, only about 5km long, is a highlight of the Upper Hollyford area, the last and highest side valley before the Homer Cirque and Homer Tunnel. It is readily accessible off the Milford Road and a popular destination for day-long summer tramps, which lead to Black Lake and Gertrude Saddle. For anyone unused to the variable colour, form and texture of alpine plants, the Gertrude is an eye-opener.

The track sets out by following a (usually) dry boulder-filled stream bed. In dry spells the stream disappears underground – a not uncommon drainage feature of the alpine zone – as it nears its confluence with the incipient Hollyford River. Silver beech forest here is patchy and the treeline uneven because of cold air draining down the valley and the impact of avalanches. With altitude, the beech trees become gnarled and stunted. In the open patches *Hoheria lyallii* is abundant, a small tree with foliage and flowers that appear too delicate for such an environment. In summer it produces masses of white honey-scented flowers amid its light-green leaves. The leaves fall in autumn, for this is one of New Zealand's few native deciduous trees.

Above the treeline the valley displays its classic glacial U-shape, sloping gently upwards. Unlike the Eglinton Valley floor on the other side of the Divide, the vegetation here – grassland, shrubland and herbfield – is composed entirely of native species. The tallest of the grasses are snow tussocks, the mid-ribbed *Chionochloa pallens* ssp *cadens* and narrow-leaved *C. rigida* ssp *amara*. Prominent among the short native grasses is the slender-leaved *Rytidosperma setifolium*.

Forming mats among the grasses and shrubs with its dark wiry branches and roundish dark-green leaves is the ubiquitous *Muehlenbeckia axillaris*. Interestingly, the petals of the small black fruits enlarge to become succulent and glassy. This plant hosts the caterpillars of two copper butterflies, *Lycaena salustius* and *L. boldenarum* which are commonly seen on warm summer days.

Prominent shrub species in the valley are *Hebe subalpina* and *H. cockayneana*, distinguished by their rounded form. The grey foliage of *Olearia moschata* and grey-green of *Brachyglottis revolutus* stand out amongst the green *Leonohebe mooreae* and whipcord *L. hectorii. Coprosma* bushes are also common, especially *C. pseudocuneata*, which generally maintains a low straggly form, and *C. serrulata*, which is quite different with its broad leathery leaves and erect form. Both carry orange-red berries. Mountain daisies are everywhere through the grassland and herbfield, the most spectacular of them being *Celmisia semicordata*. Smaller species include *C. walkeri* and *C. durietzii*.

Among the herbs are the great mountain buttercup *Ranunculus lyallii*, bearing glossy leaves the size of dinner plates, the carrot-family representatives *Anisotome flexuosa* and *A. haastii* and the speargrass *Aciphylla lyallii*, whose leaves are grass-like and difficult to distinguish from mid-ribbed snow tussock. The yellow-flowered lily *Bulbinella gibbsii balanifera* is common on the valley floor and was first described from here.

Towards the great wall at the head of the valley, the route to the saddle bears left to climb a rubbly slope leading to Black Lake. The lower section of the climb passes through low shrubland featuring pineapple shrub *Dracophyllum menziesii*. On the scree slopes and boulderfields above are the mountain shieldfern *Polystichum cystostegia*, everlasting daisy *Helichrysum bellidioides* and *Haastia sinclairii*, a trailing plant which can cope with unstable rocky slopes. Through this section the willowherb *Epilobium porphyrium* is widespread, adding little dashes of reddish purple and pink to the vegetation through its flowers and

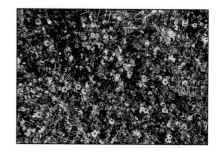

Mat-forming Muehlenbeckia axillaris, seen here fruiting, prefers stable river terraces.
All photos by Neville Peat

Celmisia verbascifolia, one of the largest of its genus of mountain daisies. The leaves are bright green and white-edged, with woolly tomentum underneath, and the flowers, up to 80mm in width, are carried on stalks over 20cm long.

The cushion daisy Celmisia hectorii, presenting light-brown seedheads in late summer.

Above: *Perched above the Gertrude Valley high in the Darran Mountains and overlooking the Upper Hollyford Valley is Black Lake.*

Left: Ranunculus lyallii, *often wrongly referred to as a lily, blooms magnificently in November/December. It is the world's largest buttercup.*

Cushions of **Kelleria croizatii** are found in the high-alpine zone of the main divide, Fiordland, Takitimu Mountains and east through northern Southland to the Lammermoor and Rock and Pillar Ranges of Otago. A member of the daphne family, it is an important host plant for many insects.

leaves. The *Dolichoglottis* daisies, formerly called *Senecio*, begin to show up here, too, and decorate the rubbly soils all the way to the saddle with their yellow, white and hybrid flowers.

Black Lake, almost circular and darkly deep, is located in a hanging valley. In winter, it freezes over. The lakebed has been scooped out by glacial ice on a step above the main valley. Bedrock surrounds the lake, scraped smooth by glaciers. Plants like glaucous *Anisotome pilifera* grow out of cracks in the rock. For the carrot-like *Anisotome*, a formidable taproot makes this possible.

Gertrude Saddle (1,430m) lies above Black Lake. A narrow shelf with a sheer drop on the western side, the saddle is home to *Poa* and other grasses (including the short snow tussock *Chionochloa oreophila*), herbs and cushion plants. The small speargrasses *Aciphylla divisa* and *A. congesta* form tufted clumps, advertising their presence with flowers that look vaguely like cauliflower heads but are pale yellow. The commonest flower is that of gentians, including *Chionogentias montana*. Cushion plants include the soft pale-green *Kelleria croizatii*; hard yellow-green *Phyllachne colensoi*, whose leaves carry little knobs; and hard whitish-green *Raoulia buchananii*, a Fiordland/western Otago endemic. Low shrubs of *Parahebe macrantha* var. *macrantha* are scattered about in rocky places below the crest, conspicuous when they produce their large snow-white flowers.

The preponderance of white flowers in the alpine flora is curious, especially as they occur in genera with distinctly different origins, distributions and reproductive arrangements. Some species with white flowers have coloured relatives overseas. Nonetheless, there is plenty of colour in the fruits – red in *Pimelea*, *Astelia*, *Gaultheria* and *Cyathodes*, pink in *Pratia* and *Gaultheria*, orange in *Nertera*, *Leucopogon* and *Podocarpus*, purple in *Myrsine* and blue or orange in *Coprosma*.

The leaves of Haastia sinclairii (*pictured here with seedheads) are insulated with dense tomentum, a woolly blanket for the cold conditions. The genus, named after Sir Julius von Haast, is endemic to New Zealand, and all three species are alpine.*

Native broom Carmichaelia arborea *in a packed herbfield. Pineapple shrub* Dracophyllum menziesii *and* Anisotome haastii *are prominent.*

Backdrop to Milford Sound

An impression of the landscape and plant life of the Cleddau Valley, from the head of the valley, where the Homer Tunnel emerges, all the way to Milford Sound.

The top two tiers illustrate the valley profile. From its steep upper reaches the valley descends steadily to a river delta at the head of Milford Sound. The main valley and side valleys were once filled

Upper Cleddau plants (from left): three-finger *Pseudopanax colensoi*; southern rata *Metrosideros umbellata*; mountain lancewood *Pseudopanax lineare*; mountain holly *Olearia ilicifolia*; koromiko *Hebe salicifolia*; mountain lacebark *Hoheria lyallii*; wineberry *Aristotelia serrata*; kiokio *Blechnum capense*; southern rata and silver beech *Nothofagus menziesii* (in background); broad-leaved cabbage-tree or toii *Cordyline indivisa*.

with glacier ice, which left features such as hanging valleys and truncated spurs. All but the tallest peaks were submerged by ice. Today, the glaciers of this region are much reduced and confined to high altitude.

The bottom tier is a botanical kaleidoscope, representing plants typical of the upper Cleddau (left side) and the middle and lower parts of the valley (right side).

Middle/lower Cleddau plants (from left): soft tree-fern *Cyathea smithii*; karamu *Coprosma lucida*; climbing rata *Metrosideros diffusa*; tree fuchsia or kotukutuku *Fuchsia excorticata*; rimu and beech forest in valley behind; lancewood or horoeka *Pseudopanax crassifolius*; mahoe *Melicytus ramiflorus*; southern rata; muttonbird shrub *Brachyglottis rotundifolia*; inaka *Dracophyllum longifolium*.

MOUNTAIN BIRDS

The birds that are most closely associated with Fiordland's mountainous North are the rock wren, kea and takahe – three species that have virtually nothing in common except an ability to live above or close to the treeline. They look quite different, they certainly behave in different ways and they belong to different orders of avifauna. Rock wren is one of New Zealand's smallest passerine birds, takahe the largest rail and flightless, and kea a highly agile and mobile parrot. All three occur in the wild only in the South Island.

> With the demise of its close relatives, the New Zealand bush wrens (the last species, the South Island bush wren, became extinct in the 1960s), the rock wren is the only surviving species of this endemic genus.

Rock wren – High flier

Rock wren *Xenicus gilviventris* is an avian anomaly, a dainty bird, just 90mm from beak to stunted tail, that spends its entire life above the treeline. It is exclusively an alpine bird, unlike the kea, which frequently utilises forest.

Found only in South Island mountains from Nelson to Fiordland, the rock wren may be seen as high as 2,500m but in Fiordland descends with the lower treeline to under 1,000m. Some birds have been reported low down on hills around Wet Jacket Arm, Dusky Sound. Prime habitat is a stable boulderfield pitched to the sun where shrubs and herbs are abundant.

Preferring only short flights, the rock wren spends much of its time flitting or hopping through boulders in search of its food – invertebrate animals such as insects and spiders, and the fruits of alpine plants. Disproportionately large feet and a long hind claw allow it to grip the smooth hard rocks.

Usually found in pairs (although a casual observer may be aware of only one bird), rock wrens allow humans a tolerably close approach and they may linger for some minutes – bobbing up and down, wing-flicking and sometimes bowing slightly with stiff legs – before carrying on across the boulders or fellfield. Often a rock wren will be heard before it is seen. It utters a high-pitched 'tsit-tsit' call, similar to that of the rifleman.

Nests are built in holes and well-vegetated banks, or in crevices draped by vegetation. Sometimes the hole is excavated by the bird using its feet. A pouch about 25cm long is woven from grasses and lined with feathers or lichens. Egg-laying (normally a clutch of two or three) occurs between September and November and both parents incubate and feed the young.

Rock wrens are distributed widely through Fiordland (and east to the Eyre Mountains). Homer Cirque, by the eastern portal of the Homer Tunnel, has a small number. These birds, together with the ones living on the Milford Track's alpine sections, probably have the most human contact. Compared to the distinctly brown rock wrens in the main part of the Southern Alps, Fiordland males have bright-green upper parts and more yellow on their sides.

A rock wren in subalpine vegetation (Celmisia walkerii and snow grass) on Centre Pass, between the Spey and Seaforth catchments.
Ian Southey

> Little is known about how rock wrens cope with the winter's heavy snowfalls and intense cold. They probably roost in nest holes or other sheltered places, where there are a few berries and insects handily placed to nibble on. They may survive heavy snowfalls by slowing their metabolism – a condition known as torpor.

Kea –Talented parrot

A robust and fearless parrot with a seemingly insatiable curiosity, the kea *Nestor notabilis* is one of the few parrots in the world that is at home in high mountains. Its haunting 'kay-aa' call, from which it gets its Maori name, is frequently heard echoing around the valleys walls and rock bluffs of Fiordland.

Groups of juvenile kea, identified by their yellow crowns, yellowish base of bill and yellow feet, are conspicuous around the Homer Tunnel area. Kea are attracted to human structures, equipment and devices, including vehicles. The cute entertainer can become a destructive nuisance, as it is in a kea's character to try to dismantle any attractive item with the aid of a powerful beak and claws.

Kea fly considerable distances for food and social contact. Their diet is essentially vegetarian – berries, leaves, buds, stems, roots – and they take a wide range of insects. Although mostly seen above the treeline, kea spend some time roosting and feeding in the forest, and their nests tend to be located in rock crevices in montane forest. Breeding usually occurs in winter, with young being reared in spring and summer.

Kea are found in the mountains from Nelson-Marlborough to southern Fiordland. Occasionally they visit coastal forest west of the main divide and they may be seen near sea level along the Fiordland coast. They are attracted to the head of Doubtful Sound and West Arm (Lake Manapouri) by human activity, and in Milford Sound kea have caused damage to radar equipment and aerials on fishing boats.

Kea get up to all sorts of pranks. At West Arm, they have been known to prise the lead off the lead-head nails used on roofing iron, carry the lead pieces to the roof top and let them skid down the corrugated iron. Seemingly they find the noise entertaining.

Important: Do not feed kea and do not leave valuable gear unattended for too long in kea territory. Treat them as a natural hazard and be thankful there are no bears about in this wild region.

A juvenile kea investigates an old stump at Big River near Fiordland's south coast.
Ian Southey

Takahe – A survivor

For the first half of the twentieth century, takahe *Porphyrio mantelli hochstetteri* were considered extinct. Then in 1948, Dr Geoffrey Orbell found numbers of them living in the Murchison Mountains west of Te Anau. The news astonished the bird world – a species had been brought back from the dead.

Takahe are flightless rails and highly colourful, with indigo head, neck and breast, a metallic green back, and red bill, legs and feet. Their colour scheme resembles the more common pukeko or swamphen of the lowlands, but there the similarity ends. For the takahe is almost three times the weight of pukeko, at 2-3.5kg (males are heavier), it stands taller and has a much stouter bill and legs. Whereas pukeko may have two or even three broods a year with five or six eggs per clutch, takake pairs breed only once a year and raise only one chick from up to three eggs laid.

Takahe are endangered. The total population, wild and captive, is only about 200. The main wild population of about 120 live mostly above the treeline in the Murchison Mountains, where they feed on snow tussock leaves (*Chionochloa rigida* ssp *amara*, *C. pallens* ssp *cadens* and *C. crassiuscula*) and the leaves of the mountain daisy *Celmisia petriei*. Only the basal portion of the leaves, the most nutritious part, is utilised, although grass seeds are eaten when available. In winter, when the tussocks are buried under snow, the birds enter the forest lower down and feed mainly on the carbohydrate-rich rhizomes of the summer-green fern *Hypolepis millefolium*, which they grub up with their powerful feet. Their diet, therefore, is highly specialised.

Pairs hold territories in the subalpine grasslands. Calls can easily be mistaken for those of weka, but are actually deeper and more piercing. Pairs sing alternating duets. Bowl-shaped nests are made from tussock leaves and shoots and the eggs are usually laid between October and December, when late snowfalls can threaten breeding.

Takahe are relatively long-lived, with some birds known to have reached more than 20 years of age. Small numbers of takahe are held on Maud, Mana, Kapiti and Tiritiri Matangi Islands and also at Mt Bruce National Wildlife Centre. The breeding pair at Te Anau Wildlife Park attracts large numbers of visitors.

Reasons for the decline of takahe over the past 100 years include competition with red deer for food and predation by stoats and ferrets. Takahe were once found through much of south-west South Island in the nineteenth century. But it is clear numbers were waning even by the time Maori arrived. The decline was possibly brought about by climate change and glacial advances that occurred over many thousands of years, reducing their habitat and making them vulnerable to extinction. A North Island race of takahe is known only from subfossil bones. In the South Island, Maori hunting of small, isolated populations may have accelerated the decline of the species as a whole.

Brown kiwi

Fiordland is a stronghold for the South Island brown kiwi *Apteryx australis*. Essentially a forest bird, brown kiwi are more common in western areas than in the east. They range into subalpine areas.

Kiwi have been recorded as far south as Preservation Inlet, but are now not found there. In fact, they are strangely absent from southern Fiordland. Kiwi do, however, occur on the larger islands of Resolution and Secretary. Although long-lived, they are slow breeders. There is concern that kiwi numbers are declining.

A helping hand

The artificial rearing of takahe at a special Department of Conservation facility near Burwood Bush has helped maintain numbers in the wild.

Spare eggs are taken from nests in the Murchison Mountains and transported by helicopter to Burwood Bush, where they are artificially incubated (30 days). In the field, eggs are exchanged between nests to ensure most pairs have at least one fertile egg. At the captive-rearing unit, chicks are fed using puppets (initially every half-hour through the day) and brooded by a fibreglass model of a parent bird that emits tape-recordings of brooding calls.

After a year, during which time they have been acclimatising outside in a fenced-off area, the young takahe are released into the mountains. Captive rearing started in 1984 and since then about 10-20 chicks a year have been reared. Over a six-year period (1987-92), captive-reared takahe were released in the Stuart Mountains to the north of the Murchison Mountains. Releases in the Stuart Mountains were discontinued, however, after it was realised the habitat was not as suitable as first thought and the birds were dispersing too widely. Since 1991, the Murchison Mountains have been the focus for releases of captive-reared takahe. Here, the birds have established well, pairing and breeding with wild takahe.

A series of very cold winters through the mid-1990s (coldest since records began in Takahe Valley in 1972) has caused losses in the wild population, but thanks to the captive rearing programme numbers have held at about 120. Numbers will need to increase to several hundred before the population reaches a reasonably secure level.

Below: *A takahe pair feeding on leaves of snow grass. The base portion of the leaves is the most nutritious.*
Dave Crouchley

Above: *The adult stoner (stonefly)
Apteryoperla illiesi (length 15-
20mm), a species endemic to
Fiordland's northern alpine
region, is active by night, running
quickly over wet rocks and
between boulders in search of a
mate. It must keep a lookout for
the long-legged migadopine
carabid beetle* Loxomeris, *which
is a predator and relatively
common in such habitats. Of the
10 species of stoneflies known
from the alpine zone, three
species are apterous (wingless) as
adults. One of them, the giant
Holcoperla angularis (length
25mm) is diurnal. Other stoneflies
may be shortwinged (for example,*
Austroperla cyrene) *or fully-
winged (*Zelandobius dugdalei*).
Alpine aquatic insects generally
live in swift waters in this region,
including waterfalls, torrents and
meltwaters. Sometimes the waterways constitute thin films of water
and algae covering granite rock.*
Brian Patrick

MIGHTY MIDGETS

As if drawing upon the magnificence of their landscape, the invertebrates of northern Fiordland are larger, more brightly coloured and
more boldy patterned than populations from drier eastern areas.

The fauna contains many widespread species, together with a size-
able collection of local endemics. Characteristically much of the fauna
is shared with the forests, shrublands, herbfields and grasslands of
western Otago and South Westland. An example is the grey and yellow jumping stoner (stonefly) *Halticoperla tara* and an undescribed
new species of giant snail *Powelliphanta*.

Forests of the south are not known for tree weta but the only species that has a distribution on both sides of Cook Strait, *Hemideina
crassidens*, is found down the West Coast as far south as Lake McKerrow
and the Hollyford River. Similarly, grasshoppers are not a conspicuous part of the grassland fauna in Fiordland but a stout grey/bright
pink species allied to *Sigaus obelisci* has small populations on Mt
Luxmore and above Homer Tunnel. This species is widely distributed in alpine areas across Otago.

Montane beech forests generally support a rich but widespread
invertebrate fauna, but shrublands and streams associated with the
forest may also harbour species that are not so cosmopolitan, such as
the caddis *Zelandopsyche ingens* and *Edpercivalia spaini*. Large stoners
are a feature of this zone, with the green and purple *Stenoperla
maclellani* (wingspan 45-60mm) and brown *Megaleptoperla grandis*
(wingspan 60mm) being common.

In contrast, at higher altitudes, short-winged or wingless stoneflies
are characteristic of seepages and torrents, for example species such
as *Apteryoperla illiesi*, *Holcoperla angularis* and *Zelandobius dugdalei*. They
are joined by the tiny black caddis *Tiphobiosis childi*, pale-brown *T.
fulva* and yellow *T. salmoni* above 900 metres, all of which have carnivorous larvae.

Megaherbfields and diverse shrublands in the upper-montane/
low-alpine zones support many colourful insects, such as a red mirid
bug *Romna bicolor* and two colourful diurnal moths of the genus
'*Dasyuris*' (*D. callicrena*, *D. fulminea*), whose larvae feed on the shrub
Hebe cockayneana. On warm summer days the green and pink cicada
Kikihia rosea sings noisily from the shrubtops while a variety of diurnal flies pollinate the many shrub and herb flowers. Flying over the
grasslands and herbfields on a warm day is the fine orange-cream
moth *Gelophaula triscula*, whose larvae bore into the stems of *Celmisia*
daisies.

Where granite scree dominates, the black-and-white moth
Orocrambus clarkei eximia and black butterfly *Percnodaimon merula* are
ubiquitous. In calm conditions the black butterfly, largest of the day-
flying *Lepidoptera* in the mountains, glides and drifts picturesquely
over the rocks.

Dark and hairy insects are typical of high-alpine areas. The black
colouration (melanin) absorbs solar energy and may protect against

ultraviolet rays, allowing the insects maximum activity during sunshine hours, which, in their short lives, may be few. Alpine flies, moths and stoners can be found above 1,800m, amongst fellfield of sparse cushion plants and short grasses.

Nocturnal activity is limited at this high altitude but a surprising variety of species can be detected below 1,000m. Typically it is the noctuid moths that pour into any light sources. Species such as the elegant *Graphania maya*, *G. oliveri* and *Aletia nobilia* are common. On a warm cloudy night, up to 120 species may be attracted to light, underlining the richness of the Fiordland fauna.

Three moths with orange underwings are often found sunbathing on Fiordland tracks. The largest *Paranotoreas brephosata* is widespread in the alpine zone; *P. zopyra* is found in montane to low-alpine areas, and *P. opipara* has only been found in the Murchison Mountains and the alpine zone of Stewart Island. When they close their dark forewings and rest on rock surfaces, these moths are well camouflaged.

Mountain tiger

One of the most conspicuous insects in northern Fiordland is the hairy orange-brown larvae of the alpine tiger moth *Metacrias erichrysa*. About 30mm long, the caterpillars may be seen crawling over bare ground in search of their favourite food plants – grasses and herbs that include *Dolichoglottis scorzoneroides*. Tiger moth caterpillars wriggling over the road east of the Homer Tunnel have even been known to stop cars and buses! The adult moths emerge in summer, although only the yellow-and-black male flies. They are seen by day frantically searching for the flightless fawn-coloured females, which are hidden under rocks in a fluffy nest, the remains of the pupal cocoon. Their immobility accounts for the way the caterpillars are often concentrated in one area.

Above: Maoricicada nigra, *a species of alpine black cicada (length 20mm, pictured), lives in the high-alpine zone of Fiordland. A related species M. oromelaena lives in low-alpine areas. As in all other New Zealand cicadas, males do most of the singing, their resonant rasping voices making good use of their amphitheatre-like surroundings. In contrast to the adults' short lifespan (about 10 days), larvae probably feed underground on plant roots for up to a decade or more.*
Brian Patrick

Below: *Among the nine species of* Notoreas *moth known from Fiordland and the Livingstone and Takitimu Mountains is the large* N. mechanitis *(pictured right, wingspan 21-24mm), which may be seen flying by day over alpine herbfields from 900 to 1,500m. Its green and pink larvae feed on* Kelleria *cushion (below, amongst the grey and large-flowered* Raoulia grandiflora *on Gertrude Saddle). One other colourful large species,* N. niphocrena, *is rare in Fiordland while three species,* N. hexaleuca, N. galaxias *and* Notoreas *new species, reach only the eastern Fiordland mountains from strongholds in Otago and Southland.*
Brian Patrick

Fiordland's northern region is a centre of diversity and endemism for diurnal moths of the *Dasyuris* genus. One of the most widespread is *D. anceps* (pictured left, wingspan 30mm), whose larvae feed on *Anisotome flexuosa*. The genus also includes *D. octans*, whose 18mm-long orange-headed black-and-white striped larvae (pictured right) feed on *Aciphylla congesta*, one of the diminutive speargrasses. If disturbed, the caterpillars fall into the centre of the rosette, where they are protected from would-be predators by the dense spines. Eight *Dasyuris* species are found in the region.

Brian Patrick

Left: *New Zealand's largest caddis* Zelandopsyche ingens *(wingspan up to 53mm) is widespread in the western South Island, including Fiordland. Larvae live within a portable protective case, 30mm long and constructed of silk, leaves and wood immersed in swift cold streams such as the tributaries of the Cleddau or Hollyford Rivers, where this adult was collected. Larvae feed on dead leaves and wood.*

Brian Patrick

Giant invertebrates on parade
Giant slug *Amphikonophora giganteus*/length 90mm
Giant wingless stoner *Holcoperla angularis*/length 25mm
Giant caddis *Zelandopsyche ingens*/wingspan 53mm
Giant weevil *Lyperobius* new species/length 25mm
Giant weta *Hemideina crassidens*/length 50-70mm
Giant moths *Aoraia aurimaculata, A. dinodes*/wingspan 70mm
Bat-winged fly *Exsul singularis*/wingspan 28mm
Giant snail *Powelliphanta spedeni*/diameter 40mm
Giant wasp *Rhyssa persuasoria*/length 55-75mm

Captain James Cook described the blackfly as 'the most mischievous animal' his crew encountered. In Maori tradition, te namu the blackfly was divinely created to prevent humans from being rendered idle by the beauty of Fiordland.

Right: *Lifecycle of the blackfly, shown anti-clockwise from top left: cluster of eggs on rock under water; five larvae attached to rocks under water, moving about and feeding on micro-organisms; pupa immobile on rock, with air bubble enclosing a newly emerging adult rising to the surface; and adult in flight above stream.*

The biting blackfly

Among New Zealand insects, no group can beat the blackfly for notoriety. Commonly called sandflies (a misnomer because they are not dependent on sandy sites), they are rife in Fiordland. There are 13 described New Zealand species in the genus *Austrosimulium*, all of which belong to the family *Simuliidae*, but only two species bite humans. *A. australense* is found throughout New Zealand; *A. ungulatum* in the South Island and Stewart Island. The various other species can still be a nuisance as they hover around or crawl over bare skin.

Surprisingly, it is only the females that bite or pay attention to humans. Males, which feed on sap, are seldom seen. Adult females seek a blood meal to obtain the protein required to produce an additional batch of eggs. The itchy feeling and local swelling is caused by the anticoagulant pumped into the victim to prevent the sucked blood from clogging the insect's proboscis. Female blackflies tend to frequent the edges of ecological areas (ecotones) where vertebrate fauna, including birds, lizards, bats and seals, often congregate. This is why blackflies are often abundant at the edge of a forest or at a beach.

Blackfly larvae are aquatic, feeding on minute organisms in a variety of stream types. The female must return to the stream to lay a raft of yellow-orange eggs under water on a rock or plant surface.

Giant weevils

Of the 20 species of giant weevil (*Molytini*) of the genera *Hadramphus* and *Lyperobius*, nine occur in the Fiordland region.

Typically adults are slow-moving and vulnerable to rats and other mammalian predators. This may explain the preponderance of existing populations in high mountains, where predators are fewer in number. *Aciphylla* or *Anisotome* species, in the carrot family (*Apiaceae*), are the main hosts.

The black *Lyperobius coxalis* (32mm) lives in the mid-eastern and southern mountains of Fiordland, notably the Hunter Mountains. One undescribed black-and-white *Lyperobius* species (20mm) is confined to alpine areas of the Takitimu Mountains while three species, *L. spedeni* (33mm), *L. cupiendus* and *L. hudsoni*, are found through central and western Otago, extending west as far as the Livingstone and Ailsa Mountains.

Two undescribed species are distributed from the Kepler or Murchison Mountains northwards to Tutoko Valley or to western Otago mountains.

Two species are found around the fiords. The knobbled weevil *Hadramphus stilbocarpae* (page 85) has been collected at Breaksea Sound and Puysegur Point as well as at Big South Cape Island (off Stewart Island) and The Snares. Larvae and adults feed on the large herb *Stilbocarpa* at southern sites but their Fiordland equivalents switch to another megaherb, *Anisotome lyallii*, a member of the carrot family, possibly because *Stilbocarpa* does not occur in Fiordland north of Chalky and Preservation Inlets, although more complex historical reasons may be involved. An undescribed *Lyperobius* species has a compact distribution in ranges between Dusky and Edwardson Sound.

Right: *An undescribed species of giant weevil, 25mm long, from Gertrude Saddle crawling amongst* Anisotome haastii, *which is the host plant for both larvae and adults.*
Brian Patrick

Left: *This extraordinary and elusive fly lives in the northern region of Fiordland – the bat-winged fly* Exsul singularis. *The adults (wingspan 28mm) are diurnal, and are usually found sunbathing on large rocks in or adjacent to streams. From these vantage points they can predate emerging aquatic insects. Although it has occasionally been found in large numbers (there are records from Homer Tunnel, Milford Track and Milford itself, where it was first described in 1901), the bat-winged fly is generally elusive. Even at known locations it appears infrequently. It is a member of the large family* Muscidae, *subfamily* Coenosiinae, *and ranges north along the mountain backbone of the South Island to the Paparoa Range.*
Brian Patrick

Giant slugs

Damp, shady rock overhangs shelter a number of very large native slugs of the family *Athoracophoridae*, including *Amphikonophora giganteus* and the one pictured right, a new species of the same genus that was found in the Darran Mountains. Four other species are known from Fiordland in the genera *Pseudaneitea* and *Athoracophorus*, some of them endemic to the region. Most are very colourful, in shades of brown, yellow or green, with a leaf-vein pattern on their backs.

Giant slugs use their radular teeth to scrape living lichens off rock surfaces. While feeding at night they may reach 90mm, but they contract to half the length while resting during the day.

Gary Barker

Giant snails

Giant land snails are not common in Fiordland, with all three known species vulnerable to extinction and found only locally.

One of the species, *'Powelliphanta' fiordlandica*, is found in the forests of Resolution Island and at the treeline of ranges south of there. It belongs to an undescribed genus. An undescribed species of *Powelliphanta* occurs from Wolf River north to Jackson Bay.

The third species, although named as a Fiordland endemic subspecies, is now considered identical to *P. spedeni* (diameter 40mm), which is distributed eastwards through the Eyre, Garvie and Umbrella Mountains as well as Mt Benger, Mataura Range and Old Man Range. In Fiordland it is known only from the Hunter Mountains/Green Lake area, where it is locally common and conspicuous. Although predatory, these snails are in turn eaten by introduced fauna such as possums and blackbirds.

A new species of native snail (diameter 37mm) in the genus Powelliphanta, *from Wolf River.*
Rhys Buckingham

FATHOMING THE FIORDS   Chapter 5
Tentacles of the sea

Other regions of New Zealand can boast snowy mountains and forested valleys, but only Fiordland has fiords. There are 14 main fiords and they occur at intervals along about 210km of curving coastline, from Milford Sound to Preservation Inlet.

Numerous arms, some four of which are named fiords, fork and radiate from the main fiords, giving the region a tentacled appearance on the maps. In particular, the three southernmost fiords, Dusky Sound, Chalky Inlet and Preservation Inlet, make deep and widespread indentations, reflecting the older and more eroded nature of the rocks of the south. The land surrounding the two big inlets is noticeably lower, less steep and more benched than in the north. Dusky, Chalky and Preservation broaden in their outer reaches and become fragmented by islands and embayments.

The fiords north of Doubtful Sound are of a different character. They tend to be non-branching fingers, high-walled and less well endowed with bays and coves. Milford Sound is a classic example. Immediately south is Poison Bay, the shortest of the fiords at 5km. The longest fiord is Dusky Sound, which extends 44km inland.

Doubtful Sound is the second longest fiord. Deep Cove, at the head, is just 40km from the open sea. Thompson and Bradshaw Sounds link with Doubtful Sound at the southeast end of Secretary Island (Bradshaw is one of the arm-like sounds). The Spanish place-names in Doubtful Sound are the legacy of a Spanish expedition, under Alessandro Malaspina, which explored the outer part of the sound in 1793, a mere 20 years after Cook.

Geographical features in Doubtful Sound include Commander Peak, which rises 900m straight out of Hall Arm, and

What's in a name?

Fiordland maps describe the large indentations along the coast as 'sounds' rather than 'fiords'.

Strictly, they are fiords. A fiord is a deep glaciated valley, typically long, narrow and steep-sided, that has been flooded by the sea following the retreat of the glaciers.

A sound is something different – a river valley flooded by the sea as a result of rising sea levels or tilting and depression of the land, or a combination of both. The Marlborough Sounds offer examples.

In Fiordland the fiords are invariably called sounds, except for the two big inlets (Chalky and Preservation) in the south. To confuse things even further, the largest arms of Lake Te Anau are called fiords even though they are some distance from the sea.

The outer reaches of Dusky Sound from
Resolution Island, with Anchor Island
the large island at centre, and the tip of
Five Fingers Peninsula in the distance
right.
Lou Sanson

Browne Falls, which tumble a total distance of just over 600m from the source at Lake Browne. Throughout the northern sounds, waterfalls are a feature. Milford has its Bowen and Stirling Falls. In Caswell Sound the 365m-high Shirley Falls cascade from Lake Shirley near the head of the 16km-long sound.

Deep basins separated by submerged sills or thresholds occur in most of the fiords. The basins occur where glacier ice was thickest. Sills were built by terminal moraines, and their spacing represents the various glacial maximums over the ice ages. Milford Sound depths exceed 300m in places, but sills of terminal moraine reduce the depth to within 100m at its seaward end.

Caswell Sound, for example, has a maximum depth of 416m but the depth at its entrance is only 143m because of sill development there. Doubtful Sound reaches a depth of 421m but is much shallower in places like Te Awaatu Channel (The Gut). Shoreline length of the main fiords totals about 1,000km, and together the fiord walls cover some 46 sq km.

Where sea has flooded land, estuaries often form. But in the fiords of Fiordland estuarine conditions are rare. Life here takes on extraordinary form and meaning.

Fiord no more
Lake McKerrow (see photo, page 55) is a fiord cut off from the sea. At 15km in length and 2.2km wide, it has the classic form of a fiord but it is now separated from the sea at Martins Bay by 2.4km of moraines, outwash gravels and sand dunes.

Sutherland Sound, 25km south of Milford, is a fiord in transformation. A build-up of sand and mud in its outer reaches is threatening to isolate the 3km inner basin of the fiord.
Peter Johnson

LIFE UNDER WATER

Of all the ecosystems in Fiordland, the strangest is surely the underwater world of the fiords.

A conspicuous clue to the irregular nature of this environment is the absence of species that are common in the intertidal zone of rocky shores elsewhere in southern New Zealand. Blue mussels, barnacles and seaweeds, especially the green sea lettuce (*Ulva* species) are usually found in profusion along rocky coasts, but here the fringing rocks carry rather fewer species. In many places the rock is bare.

The reason for this, and for even more unusual patterns below the tide line, is the phenomenon of a fresh-water layer riding on the surface of the sea within the fiords. Although the fiords are, of course, open to the sea, wave action is restricted and the fresh-water layer is not mixed to any great degree with the sea water below, especially in the upper reaches of the fiords.

The tidal range is only moderate in the fiords (2.6m for mean spring tides, 2m for mean neap tides) and tidal currents are not pronounced. Strong currents have been measured only over the sills at some fiord entrances.

Sea water at the bottom of deep basins separated by shallow sills can remain undisturbed for long periods in some fiords. The movement of water in the fiords has been calculated by measuring dissolved oxygen, which is consumed at a natural rate by biological respiration. From these tests, it is possible to tell how long a body of water has remained stagnant. Sea temperatures average 11 degrees Celsius and reach a maximum of only 15 degrees – the smallest annual range anywhere on the New Zealand coast. Temperature decreases slightly with depth, and in the deepest basins it remains a uniform 11 or 12 degrees.

A critical factor in underwater life, one which dictates the vertical boundaries for plant and animal communities, is the availability of light. The fresh-water or low-salinity layer restricts it, but so, too, do the high walls, which in the northern zone commonly rise at angles of 60 to 80 degrees – that is, not far off perpendicular. Thus the walls cast long shadows, even in the middle of summer. In winter, large areas of water are shaded all day.

As a result of these factors, the fiords constitute a haven for animals that are dark-adapted, slow-growing and usually associated with deep water, for example certain sponge, coral, gorgonian fan and sea pen species. Several animals collected previously only from the continental shelf at depths of 100-200m turn up commonly in the fiords in water less than 30m. They include red and pink hydrocorals, shrimps, sponges, sea pens, certain seastars (starfish) and orange-lined perch, making the fiords a favourite place for divers.

The dominant animals in the upper 5m – that is, within the

Fresh-water lens

When fresh water meets the sea in the fiords, it forms a layer of low salinity on the top three to five metres.

Unless it is mixed with the sea water through current or wave action the fresh water, being less dense, will ride on the surface.

In a high-rainfall zone like Fiordland, rivers, streams, waterfalls and rain falling directly on the fiords together ensure the fresh-water layer is continuously replenished. Although the sediment load is low because of the hardness of the rocks, the inflow is stained by tannin, humic acid and dissolved organic material picked up from the forest leaf litter.

As a result, the low-salinity layer is the colour of pale ale or weak tea. It becomes a coloured lens, allowing only a dim yellow-green light to penetrate through to a gloomy world below. Light levels at 10m in the fiords are equivalent to those at 70m in the open sea.

In the rare times of drought (10 days without rain could constitute a drought), the lens becomes clearer and more light penetrates. Phytoplankton blooms are a possibility at such times.

In winter and spring, temperatures in the upper layer are a few degrees cooler than in the sea below, especially when the fiords are receiving meltwater during spring thaws.

low-salinity lens and close in underneath it – are cushion stars, tubeworms, and mussels. At depths of 5-15m the walls are encrusted with tubeworms, sponges, soft corals, colonial sea squirts and file shells. Predators of these animals include starfish, urchins, rock lobsters and snails.

Below 15m, gloom sets in. The water is calm and clear. Tubeworms are replaced by sponges, sea squirts, red and pink hydrocorals, black coral colonies, gorgonians, sea pens and brachiopods and bryozoan lace corals.

Fish are commonest in the upper 40m. About 50 species have been recorded. Red and blue cod, tarakihi and sea perch are plentiful. And orange-lined perch is one of the deep-water species found in relatively shallow water in the fiords.

Then there are species new to science – some snails, sea anemones, sponges and corals. Fiordland's black coral, *Antipathes fiordensis*, turned out to be a new species and was given an appropriate name.

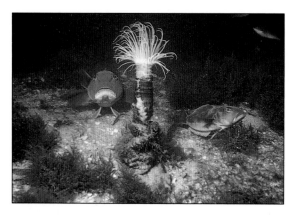

Two blue cod, sea-floor dwellers mainly, patrol a tube anemone (cerianthid) which fishes food with tentacles armed with stinging cells that act like tiny harpoons.
Lance Shaw (above and below)

The brachiopod Terebratella sanguinea *is common and colourful in the fiords.*
Ken Grange (above and below)

Feather stars or crinoids are marine animals with an ancestry going back several hundred million years. They unfurl fern-like tentacles to trap food particles.

An orange-lined perch Lepidoperca tasmanica *in Cunaris Sound, off Chalky Inlet, at a depth of 26m.*

Black coral

Exploited throughout the Pacific for jewellery, black coral colonies are mostly found at depths over 30m. Fiordland's endemic species *Antipathes fiordensis* is different. It grows in relatively shallow water (as shallow as 5m) because of the light-absorbing fresh-water layer. And among the 150 species around the world it forms probably the largest known population – over seven million colonies.

Antipathes fiordensis grows especially well at a depth of about 15m, where it crowds the near-vertical walls. In common with overseas species, it forms colonies that in places resemble small to medium-sized trees – a shape designed to maximise feeding opportunities. Measured by annual rings, growth rates are slow, mostly less than 20mm a year. Trees over 5m tall are estimated to be at least 300 years old.

Black corals are misnamed, being neither black nor true corals. Living trees may be yellow, orange, green or white (as in *A. fiordensis*). Only the dead skeleton is black. True corals are built of calcium carbonate; black coral skeletons, made of protein reinforced with chiton, are similar in composition to an insect's cuticle.

Sediment poses a threat to black coral colonies because their living organisms, tiny polyp animals, are unable to retract and are liable to be smothered. Floods are potentially catastrophic and landslides will easily cut a swathe through a population as the rocks and trees plummet down the steep sides.

Black corals are fully protected in New Zealand. They are listed on the Convention for the International Trade in Endangered Species (CITES).

'Living fossil'

Brachiopods or lampshells are the most ancient of filter-feeding shellfish, with fossils dating back an astonishing 500 million years.

Once dominant on the sea floor, brachiopods are not nearly so common today. They appear to have been displaced by faster-growing, more adaptable bivalve molluscs.

Fiordland's brachiopod communities, containing at least five species, may be as abundant as any around the world. In Goose Cove, between Five Fingers Peninsula and Resolution Island, four brachiopod species have been found inhabiting the same area – *Terebratella sanguinea*, which is red and fluted and perhaps the commonest species (photo, left), *Calloria inconspicua*, *Notosaria nigricans* and *Liothyrella neozelandica*. In parts of Preservation Inlet, these four species – plus *Neothyris lenticularis*, the largest – occur in close proximity.

Symbiosis

A serpent or snake star *Astrobrachion constrictum* uncoiled on black coral. Found only on black coral, the species feeds mainly on mucus produced by the polyps but it also feeds on plankton, including copepods, captured by the coral. In turn, the serpent star's feeding movements clear the coral of floating sediment and detritus.

The star has five arms, each up to 50cm long. In the gloom of day the star coils its arms tightly; by night, however, it will extend its arms in order to feed. The larger coral colonies play host to numerous stars, which often differ in colour. Some stars hardly move. One star was observed on the same place on its coral over a period of eight years. One black coral colony, 2.5m tall, had 18 attached to it.

Ken Grange

MARINE MAMMALS

The subdued waters of the fiords attract numerous marine mammals – dolphins, whales and seals. Dolphins, favourites with visitors because of their boat-chasing antics, are generally encountered in pods or family groups.

Pods of bottlenose dolphin *Tursiops truncatus*, up to 60 strong, inhabit Milford and Doubtful Sounds. Up to 4m in length, they have short stout beaks, grey backs grading to a white belly, and a hooked dorsal fin. Besides riding the bow waves of boats, they often perform spectacular leaps and somersaults.

Bottlenose dolphins sometimes swim up the tidal stretch of the Hollyford River to Lake McKerrow, perhaps in pursuit of trout. From studies done elsewhere, it is presumed that deepwater fish such as hoki, and squid, figure largely in their diet.

Pods of dusky dolphin *Lagenorhynchus obscurus* are also found in the fiords. The common dolphin *Delphinus delphis* is more likely to be seen offshore than in the fiords. Both species enjoy riding bow waves, although dusky dolphins spend less time at this activity.

Common dolphins, up to 2.1m long, congregate in large herds, sometimes mixing with dusky dolphins. The black beak is long and narrow, the dorsal fin noticeably tall. The flanks exhibit a criss-cross colour pattern of grey and light tan, with the back a combination of dark blue and grey.

Dusky dolphins, up to 2m long, are best known for their high leaping and backward somersaults. Their heads are pointed – they have virtually no beak – and the dorsal fin is upright. Back and tail are bluish black.

There are no known populations of Hector's dolphin, smallest of all dolphins, in the fiords, but they do occur at Te Waewae Bay (page 109).

Whales are sometimes seen in Fiordland's coastal waters, although they are more common around Foveaux Strait – an old whaling ground. These days a whale sanctuary exists south of latitude 40 degrees south. Southern right, humpback and sperm whales, which reach 16-18m in length, have all been recorded off Fiordland, with southern right whales most commonly seen. There have also been sightings of orca or killer whale *Orcinus orca*. Bearing tall and prominent dorsal fins, they are strikingly black and white and grow to about 9m in length. One or more species of beaked whale possibly visit the fiords. The only clue to date has been the recording of unidentified low-frequency clicks in Doubtful Sound.

Among the seals, the New Zealand fur seal is by far the most numerous species (see box). Elephant seals lumber ashore occasionally. Visits by leopard seals from their subantarctic haunts are rare and most likely in winter.

Fur Seals

Fully protected now following near-extinction on the mainland in the early 1800s, the New Zealand fur seal *Arctocephalus forsteri* is making a dramatic comeback. The Fiordland and south Westland populations are increasing and are probably reinforcing colonies in other parts of the South Island.

There are breeding colonies scattered along the Fiordland coast, with the largest (an estimated 5,000 seals) located on the Solander Islands. For breeding habitat, fur seals favour sea caves and rocky shelves out of reach of waves. Haul-out sites include rock islets, gravel beaches and vegetated shores (turf or tussock).

From late October breeding males, up to 1.8m long and 160kg in weight, set up territories and fight hard to hold them. Females give birth in December, mating with the territory-holder about a week later. The pup is dependent on its mother for almost a year.

Arrow squid and octopus figure largely in the diet of fur seals, which feed mainly at night. Diving to over 200m, they also eat fish, mainly hoki, barracouta and lanternfish.

Maori hunted fur seals in pre-European times but the main hunting pressure came from European sealers, who followed up reports from Captain Cook and other explorers that southern New Zealand had a rich resource in fur seals, whose dense grey-brown coat was the main product sought by the sealers.

Hooker's sea lion *Phocarctos hookeri*, whose main breeding colonies are in the subantarctic Auckland Islands, is also making a comeback on mainland New Zealand but in smaller numbers. Sea lions are occasional visitors to southern Fiordland. Haul-out sites include the Solander Islands.

Above: *Bottlenose dolphins displaying on Doubtful Sound, where pods of 40 to 60 dolphins are reasonably common. Long-term studies of these dolphins are being carried out by Otago University marine scientists.*
Steve Dawson

Several short-tailed bats flew into the sails of *HMS Clio* in Milford Sound in 1871 during a cruise of the sounds by Governor Sir George Bowen. No sightings of short-tailed bats have been reported from Fiordland since then.

Right: *The Nee Islands at the entrance to Doubtful Sound support large numbers of New Zealand fur seals.*
Neville Peat

SEA BIRDS

The fiords provide breeding habitat for a range of sea birds, some resident, some migratory.

Three species of shag or cormorant in the genus *Phalacrocorax* breed in the region – pied, black and little. The black-and-white pied shag or karuhiruhi is distinguished from little shag by its larger size and its patch of yellow above the bill. It nests in trees, typically southern rata. Little and black shags are found on inland waterways as well as at estuaries. Black shag, largest of the New Zealand cormorants (88cm from bill to tail), nests in trees and also in tussocks and on cliff ledges.

Most common of the migratory birds is the sooty shearwater *Puffinus griseus*, better known as muttonbird or titi. Colonies occur mostly in the southern fiords, especially Dusky Sound, and mostly on islands. In spring, sooty shearwaters migrate south from the North Pacific in their millions, with small islands off Stewart Island and The Snares harbouring the most numerous colonies. Each pair raises a single chick. Stewart Island populations are the target of muttonbirders, who take the chicks just before fledging (April/May). Elsewhere, the species is protected.

Other tube-nosed sea birds (*Procellariiformes*) breeding in Fiordland are broad-billed prion *Pachyptila vittata* and mottled petrel *Pterodroma inexpecta*. Broad-billed prion or parara, which is common in southern New Zealand waters and the South Atlantic, was first described in 1777 from specimens taken from Anchor Island, Dusky Sound, by George Forster, a scientist with Cook. There is a colony based at the islets off Five Fingers Peninsula, adjacent to Anchor Island, and burrows on several islets south of Anchor Island. Other breeding sites have been recorded in Breaksea Sound (Hawea Island and an islet near Oliver Point) and at a headland near Nancy Sound. The bill of this species, bearing a comb-like fringe, is remarkable – almost as wide at its base as the bird's head. It is used to strain zooplankton.

> ### Penguins
> Two penguin species inhabit the fiords – Fiordland crested penguin *Eudyptes pachyrhynchus* and blue penguin *Eudyptula minor*. The former, standing 40cm tall and weighing about 3kg, is one of the world's rarest species. The total population (south Westland, Fiordland and Stewart Island) was estimated in the mid-1990s at 2,500. In Fiordland, most Fiordland crested penguins nest on islands, with one of the largest populations occurring on Breaksea Island and small adjacent islands (215 nests, 425 birds counted in 1992).
>
> Blue penguins (korora), which are more widely distributed (throughout New Zealand, Chatham Islands and southern Australia) and more numerous, are the world's smallest penguins, weighing little more than 1kg. They usually nest in burrows. In Fiordland most colonies are found from Doubtful Sound south. Usually each pair raises two chicks and in good years there will be a good clutch.

Left: *A sooty shearwater on a feeding dive in one of the fiords at a depth of about 20m. They swim with powerful strokes of their flexed wings.*
Lance Shaw

Right: *A pair of brown skuas* Catharacta skua lonnbergi *at Hawea Island near the entrance to Breaksea Sound. They mostly breed on islands south of the New Zealand mainland, but there are possibly a few breeding on the Fiordland coast.*
Peter Johnson

Right: *White-capped or shy molly-mawks breed on New Zealand subantarctic islands (The Snares, Bounty and Auckland Islands) and frequently fly the seas off Fiordland. They are the largest of the mollymawks, with a wingspan of 2.5m.*
Wynston Cooper

Right: *Fiordland crested penguins nest in low coastal forest up to about 30m from the shore. Nest sites may be among boulders, in caves, burrows or hollows under tree roots. Males have a larger bill and body. Breeding starts in July. Usually two eggs are laid but only one chick will be reared. While the parents are at sea feeding, the chicks assemble in creches. Squid is the staple prey item, but krill and fish are also taken. Fledging generally occurs in November. In autumn, Fiordland crested penguins go to sea for a few months.*
Ian Southey

Mottled petrel (korure) breed in Dusky Sound (Front Islands in Bowen Channel and Shag Islands in Paget Passage) and also in Preservation Inlet (an islet in Isthmus Sound). There are also colonies at Lake Hauroko (page 95) and the Solander Islands (page 89).

New Zealand's three gull species are all found in Fiordland – black-backed, red-billed and black-billed – and two oyster-catcher species, South Island pied and variable. The variable (black) oystercatcher is more numerous.

Although albatrosses rarely enter the fiords, they are frequently seen off the Fiordland coast. Southern Buller's mollymawk is the most commonly encountered species, with a major colony located at the Solander Islands. Mollymawk is a term used in New Zealand and Australia to describe certain albatross species.

ISLANDS Home away from home?

The fiords contain several hundred islands, ranging in size from Resolution Island (20,870ha) to numerous shrub-topped islets with room enough only for a handful of seabird burrows. Not only do the islands add mystery and charm to the landscape of the fiords; some of them are biological gems – havens for fauna and flora that struggle to compete with introduced predators and browsing animals.

Separating Breaksea and Dusky Sounds, Resolution Island, 20km by 12km, is New Zealand's second largest inshore island (after Great Barrier). Five Fingers Peninsula is attached to it by a narrow stretch of mud and sand. The second largest island in Fiordland, and New Zealand's fifth largest inshore island, is Secretary Island (8130ha), which lies boot-shaped between the entrances of Doubtful and Thompson Sounds.

Rising to over 1,000m, these two large islands are largely covered by beech forest that gives way to flowering trees and shrubs at the edges. Both islands have been invaded by deer and stoats. There are rats and mice on Resolution Island but, surprisingly, none on Secretary Island. Both are apparently possum-free. There are brown kiwi and western weka populations on both islands, and a resident kaka population on Resolution Island.

Below: *Breaksea Island from the ocean side, with Hawea and Wairaki at centre right. Hawea is the larger. Silver beech trees at the summit of Breaksea are over 20m tall. Mountain beech is mixed with silver beech on the upper slopes, with rata and kamahi dominating the lower slopes. Exposed ridges are covered in mahoe,* Dracophyllum longifolium *and kiekie, with tree ferns appearing in shaded gullies. The coastal shrubs include* Olearia oporina, *inaka* Dracophyllum longifolium *and* Hebe elliptica.

Neville Peat

Above: *Knobbled weevil* Hadramphus stilbocarpae *(22mm long), pictured here on its food plant,* Anisotome lyallii. *In addition to this species, Breaksea Island has a population of an elegant large brown weevil, a new species in the genus* Anagotus, *whose adults and larvae both feed on* Olearia oporina. *The species is also found in the Cameron Mountains northeast of Preservation Inlet.*

Peter Johnson

Island sanctuaries

Several islands are refuges for endangered fauna and have been accorded the highest conservation status. Four near the entrance to Breaksea Sound – Breaksea, Hawea, Wairaki and an islet known as OG3 – have 'special area' status. They are considered to be beyond the swimming range of stoats or rats. Other islands of high value are Nee and Shelter Islands (Doubtful Sound), an unnamed island in Dusky Sound, and the Solander Islands.

At least 40 other islands are designated open sanctuaries or islands with potential to be cleared of pests and turned into refuges for threatened birds and invertebrates. The largest is Chalky Island (475ha) at the entrance to Chalky Inlet. A trapping programme to clear Chalky Island of stoats was initiated in 1996.

Breaksea Island – A modern Ark

Breaksea Island (170ha), at the entrance to Breaksea Sound, is Fiordland's most prized refuge – a modern Noah's Ark.

Several endangered or vulnerable species have been transferred to Breaksea since the eradication of Norway rats through an intensive poisoning programme (1988-1991).

Breaksea, steep and densely vegetated with some 50 woody species, is the largest island in Fiordland without stoats. It is too far from the mainland – or a stepping-stone island – for them to swim to. But it did have several thousand Norway rats *Rattus norvegicus* on it until recent times – introduced possibly by sealing vessels about the turn of the nineteenth century.

The eradication of rats paved the way for the introduction of at-risk bird species. In March 1992, 59 South Island saddlebacks *Philesturnus carunculatus carunculatus* from the Stewart Island area were landed by helicopter and released. They began breeding soon afterwards and remain the only population surviving beyond offshore islands around Stewart Island. A survey of their numbers in 1996 showed the population had more than doubled. In October 1995, there was another transfer of endangered birds – 30 yellowheads or mohua (15 pairs) from the Blue Mountains in Otago.

Two endangered weevil species have been transferred to Breaksea from two small low-lying islands nearby – Wairaki and OG3 (they were formerly known as the Outer Gilbert Islands, a group that includes Hawea, the largest island, which is forested). Forty knobbled weevil *Hadramphus stilbocarpae*, a south-west New Zealand endemic, came from OG3 and 20 individuals of another weevil species, *Anagotus fairburni*, were collected from Wairaki and released on Breaksea in 1990.

The traffic was not all one-way, however. Twelve South Island robins from Breaksea were transferred to Hawea in 1987 (just in case rat poison affected this important western population). Some banded birds were seen back on Breaksea subsequently. Breaksea has good numbers of South Island robin in particular, but also of bellbird, South Island fantail, grey warbler, New Zealand pigeon, kaka and morepork. New Zealand falcon and kea have been recorded here.

Over the years rats eradicated the Fiordland skink *Oligosoma acrinasum* from Breaksea but they have been able to recolonise the island from inshore rock stacks following the removal of the rats. Forty individuals from Wairaki's large population, prospering in a rat-free environment, have been transferred to Hawea Island.

Breaksea Island and its small outliers were created a special area in June 1993. It is off-limits to the public in case of accidental introduction of rodents.

Fiordland skink

The Fiordland skink *Oligosoma acrinasum* is a local endemic, known from islands at the entrances to Breaksea, Dusky, Doubtful and Nancy Sounds, and from Coal River mouth on the mainland coast. It was identified as a new species in 1977.

Active by day, Fiordland skinks are usually found either on large rocks (with crevices for hiding) or on boulder beaches littered with driftwood and seaweed. Their habitat is often exposed to sea spray. Up to 20cm long, they are glossy black or dark brown on their back and flanks, with yellow or green flecks on the back. Communal basking is not uncommon and they have been seen intertwining at basking sites. They feed on a wide range of invertebrates – flies (including blackflies), weevils, spiders, caterpillars, wasps and small snails. There is a theory that these skinks, the only species occupying the littoral zone in Fiordland, are attracted to fur seal colonies because of a richer invertebrate fauna at such sites. Fiordland skinks can swim. They have been observed to dive into brackish splash pools and have managed to recolonise rat-free Breaksea Island by swimming from adjacent rock stacks. They utter a high-pitched squeak that is just audible to the human ear. Young are born live – up to six at a time. Stoats and rats are thought to be major predators of Fiordland skinks. At the southern end of Coal River bay, a stoat was observed with a Fiordland skink in its mouth. *Peter Johnson*

Lizards of Fiordland

Besides the Fiordland skink, the region has four other skink species (genus *Oligosoma*) and two geckos (genus *Hoplodactylus*). Despite the size of Fiordland, lizard records are sparse and much research remains to be done.

The striped skink *O. nigriplantare polychroma* (16cm) inhabits tussock grasslands in the Hunter Mountains and adjacent ranges between Lakes Monowai and Manapouri. It is also on the Mt Luxmore tops and Eglinton Valley. The larger green skink, *O. chloronoton* (20cm), is found in bouldery shrubland and tussock grassland on the more open eastern side of Lake Te Anau, north of the control gates at the lake outlet.

A new species of *Oligosoma* occurs at Big Bay and north to Awarua Point. It inhabits boulders behind the beach. A fourth skink, *O. inconspicuum*, is thought to occur in south-east Fiordland, south of Manapouri.

The two gecko species from the region are forest dwellers – *H. granulatus*, which prefers western forest and shrubland, even alpine shrubland, and has been recorded in the Sinbad and Esperance Valleys; and a form of the common gecko *H. maculatus* that has been found in red beech forest in the Eglinton Valley and near the Te Anau control gates.

The woody climber kiekie *Freycinetia baueriana banksii, which adds a tropical touch to the vegetation, reaches its natural southern limit on Five Fingers Peninsula. The white bracts, sweet and crisp, were eaten by early Maori, who also utilised the fibrous leaves in plaiting (kiekie belongs to the same family as pandanus, which is widely used in the South Pacific). The leaves can grow to 1.5m long. Although usually rooted on tree trunks, kiekie growing beside streams produce underwater roots up to a metre long.*

Chris Rance

Above: *Sweet-scented* Pimelea gnidia *is a common shrub on the Fiordland coast, growing to a height of about 2m. The species has a disjunct distribution. The nearest population is in north-east South Island.*

Chris Rance

Endemic weta

A ground weta *Zelandosandrus fiordensis* (length 35mm) is found only in forests in the outer reaches of the fiords.

COASTAL PLANTS A surprise package

The coastal vegetation of Fiordland is luxuriant and full of surprises. There is a crossroads flavour to it.

Because of the relative mildness of the climate at sea level several northern species reach their southern limit in Fiordland.

Some examples: Hutu *Ascarina lucida*, common on the West Coast, reaches as far south as Te Oneroa in Preservation Inlet; pigeonwood *Hedycarya arborea* extends to the mouth of the Waitutu River; the climbing rata *Metrosideros fulgens* makes it to West Cape and *M. perforata* reaches Catseye Bay; and the epiphytic puka *Griselinia lucida* extends to John O'Groats River.

Conversely, several southern New Zealand endemics extend northwards around the Fiordland coast. *Pimelea lyallii* grows on dunes as far north as Te Whara Beach. The megaherb *Anisotome lyallii* reaches Big Bay, and two other megaherbs, *Stilbocarpa lyallii* and *Urtica australis*, have their only South Island sites on a few islands in Preservation and Chalky Inlets.

Other distinctive features of the vegetation include the presence of the southern eyebright *Euphrasia repens* on Secretary Island but elsewhere only on Stewart Island, and the southern Southland coast. Two large daisy species, both endemic to Fiordland, decorate the coastline in places. *Olearia oporina*, with its large yellow-centred flowers, is strictly coastal and occurs north to the Kaipo River, while the herbaceous *Celmisia holosericea* dots steep coastal cliffs but is also found in alpine grasslands.

In addition to the zone of grasses, herbs and shrubs, coastal forest harbours a number of special plants. The Fiordland endemic *Carex pleiostachys* is found as far north as Yates Point, while the fern *Grammitis rigida* reaches Milford Sound and the hook-sedge *Uncinia aucklandica* ranges as far as Cascade River. A larger sedge, *Cyperus ustalatus*, plentiful in the north, reaches its southern limit at Poison Bay.

Southern rata *Metrosideros umbellata* is common right along the coast, causing the vegetation to blush heartily when in flower. Rata is often associated with kamahi, whose creamy racemes turn rusty red in late summer. Other prominent trees or shrubs are broadleaf, mahoe, muttonbird shrub, inaka *Dracophyllum longifolium*, three-finger and *Hebe elliptica*.

A slender herb of pakihi wetland, *Bulbinella modesta* has an interesting disjunct distribution. It is found between Buller and Okarito, with a gap until the Fiordland population starts at Martins Bay. A nationally rare aquatic species, *Myriophyllum robustum*, has some of its most important and secure populations in Fiordland. The feathery water milfoil occurs at lagoons and on lake margins as far south as Lake Forster, directly inland from West Cape.

Most of the sounds have small areas of saltmarsh or estuarine vegetation. Usually it is dominated by jointed rush

Leptocarpus similis, flax, saltmarsh ribbonwood *Plagianthus divaricatus* and another small-leaved shrub, *Coprosma propinqua*. Accompanying turf consists of widespread species such as sea primrose *Samolus repens*, remuremu *Selliera radicans*, *Lilaeopsis novaezelandiae*, arrow grass *Triglochin striata*, *Isolepis cernua*, *Crassula moschata* and *C. helmsii*.

Above: *A small pink-flowered shrub* Sprengelia incarnata *was discovered in Fiordland as recently as 1967. Occurring also in Tasmania, it is locally common in peaty wetlands of south-west Fiordland, such as those on top of Five Fingers Peninsula where this plant is pictured. It is an epacrid shrub (family Epacridaceae), a name which refers to its habit of growing 'on the top' of hills.*
Peter Johnson

Anisotome lyallii *flowering prolifically among boulders near the shores of Breaksea Island.*
Peter Johnson

The tree daisy Olearia oporina, *a Fiordland endemic, flowering in early summer on the Five Fingers Peninsula shoreline. It is a common shrub on the south-west Fiordland coast, growing to a height of about 3m.*
Brian Patrick

Right: *The sand-binding sedge pingao* Desmoschoenus spiralis *doing its work at Spit Island, Preservation Inlet.*
Lou Sanson

Sand milkweed Euphorbia glauca, *one of New Zealand's most threatened coastal plants, has its largest and most secure populations at six Fiordland sites. The species is also found on Norfolk Island. It has stems up to a metre long. As its species name suggests, the soft foliage is blue-green. The flowers are deep red.*

Chris Rance

Solander Islands – Precious outliers

High, angular and crowded with seabirds, the Solander Islands 40km off the south coast comprise a special protected area of Fiordland National Park. They guard the western entrance to Foveaux Strait, and they are among the least modified off-shore islands in the New Zealand region.

There are two main islands – Solander (100ha, 340m high) and Little Solander (8ha, 180m high) – and numerous rock stacks and islets. They constitute the remnants of a highly-eroded andesitic volcano. Little Solander is 2km west of the larger island.

Fifty-five vascular plants have been recorded on Solander Island, but only five woody species – a reflection of environmental factors and isolation. A dense shrubland, up to 6m high, of *Olearia lyallii* and *Brachyglottis stewartiae* dominates the summit plateau, with the megaherb *Stilbocarpa lyallii* forming a luxuriant understorey. Steep slopes support the muttonbird shrub *Brachyglottis rotundifolia* and *Hebe elliptica*, together with a variety of ferns, including *Asplenium obtusatum*. Exposed slopes are covered in grasses such as *Poa foliosa* and *P. astonii*, which are associated with the herbs Stewart Island forget-me-not *Myosotis rakiura*, Cook's scurvy grass *Lepidium oleraceum*, *Anistome lyallii* and iceplant *Dysphyma australe*.

Little Solander, on the other hand, has just 14 vascular plants, the most prominent being *Brachyglottis stewartiae*, *Hebe elliptica* and *Poa astonii*. Curiously, the megaherb *Stilbocarpa robusta*, otherwise confined to The Snares, replaces *S. lyallii* on Little Solander. Cook's scurvy grass has also found a refuge here from introduced browsing animals.

The vegetation of both islands is greatly affected by the peaty soils, climatic factors (wind and salt spray) and the space occupied by sea birds and fur seals. The blanket peat offers prime burrowing habitat for a diverse collection of sea birds.

A total of 38 species of sea and land birds have been recorded for the Solanders. Southern Buller's mollymawk *Diomedea bulleri* is the feature bird. An estimated 4,000-5,000 pairs nest on Solander Island, on pedestals of mud-caked grasses and other vegetation. They make up almost half of the total population of this subspecies (the other half breed on The Snares). Up to 300 pairs may nest on Little Solander. When not breeding these mollymawks range widely through the southern ocean, flying as far as feeding grounds off South America. With a wingspan of about 2m, they are one of the smaller mollymawk species.

The Solanders, especially Little Solander, are also notable for their colonies of common diving petrel *Pelecanoides urinatrix*, which nest in burrows in peat. In summer, each pair raises a single chick. Non-migratory, these small birds dive for krill fairly close to land and use both wings and feet for propulsion under water.

Little Solander has the southernmost colonies of Australasian gannet *Morus serrator* in New Zealand. The larger colony, comprising some 20 to 30 nests, is on the northern ridge about 80m above the sea. These large birds, with a wingspan of 2m, are renowned for their swift vertical dives for fish from heights of 20-30m. They raise a single chick over summer and disperse north after the breeding season. Banded birds in the North Island have lived to over 30 years.

Stewart Island weka *Gallirallus australis scotti* were introduced to Solander Island by sealers in the early 1800s, presumably as a food resource. They have probably caused burrowing petrel colonies on Big Solander to decline as weka are known to prey on

Leech
Little Solander Island is one of the few places in New Zealand where terrestrial leeches live. The species *Ornithobdella edentula* is also found on The Snares. Another species occurs on Open Bay Islands off South Westland, and possibly a third lives on Big South Cape Island off Stewart Island. Leeches feed on penguins and burrowing sea birds, concentrating on their feet. After a meal of blood, they greatly increase in size. These and a species from southern Victoria, Australia, are the only known representatives of the leech family *Ornithobdellidae*.

Below: *A southern Buller's mollymawk on its nest. The single egg is incubated by both parents, who return to the same nest every year. Breeding is spread over much of the year, with eggs most likely in February and chicks fed through the winter months. In contrast, northern Buller's mollymawks in the Chatham Islands lay in October-November and fledge their chicks in June.*
Wynston Cooper

Solanders' breeding sea birds
Fiordland crested penguin (pokotiwha) *Eudyptes pachyrhynchus*
Buller's mollymawk *Diomedea bulleri*
Sooty shearwater (titi) *Puffinus griseus*
Broad-billed prion (parara) *Pachyptila vittata*
Fairy prion (titi wainui) *Pachyptila turtur*
Mottled petrel (korure) *Pterodroma inexpecta*
Common diving petrel (kuaka) *Pelecanoides urinatrix*
Brown skua (hakoakoa) *Cartharacta skua lonnbergi*
Australasian gannet (takapu) *Morus serrator*
Southern black-backed gull (karoro) *Larus dominicanus*
Red-billed gull (tarapunga) *Larus novaehollandiae scopulinus*
Variable oystercatcher (toreapango) *Haematopus unicolor*
White-fronted tern (tara) *Sterna striata*

Possibly breeding
Blue penguin (korora) *Eudyptula minor*

Above: *Solander Island, viewed from Little Solander. The islands were named by James Cook in 1770 in honour of one of his scientists, the Swedish botanist Dr Daniel Solander. The Maori name for Solander Island, Hautere, means 'rushing wind'.*
Wynston Cooper

Below: *Punui* Stilbocarpa lyallii *flowering on Solander Island.*
Wynston Cooper

their chicks and eggs. Weka may have also extinguished banded rail *Rallus philippensis assimilis* on Big Solander because no rails have been recorded there in recent times, although they do exist on Little Solander.

Bush birds are reasonably common. There are populations of bellbird, grey warbler, South Island fantail, South Island tomtit and silvereye. New Zealand pigeon has been recorded. Introduced species include greenfinch, redpoll, starling, hedge sparrow, song thrush and blackbird. Red-crowned parakeets (kakariki) appear to have displaced a small population of yellow-crowned parakeets between the 1940s and the 1970s.

THE SOUTH
Last frontier

South of a line between the Kepler Mountains and Doubtful Sound, the ranges are generally of lesser height. But that is not to say the region is a walkover for overlanders. Far from it. Fiordland's south-west quarter is a crumpled and confusing landscape of intertwined ridges, extensively forested, dotted with lakes, ribboned with rivers and incised by the most complex of the fiords – Preservation and Chalky Inlets, and Dusky and Breaksea Sounds.

The South is so remote, wild and unmodified, it is capable of turning up more than a few natural history surprises – new records certainly, and possibly new species or subspecies of insects or plants. How many invertebrate animals await discovery – snails, beetles, spiders and so on? What about birds? Are the South's forests concealing the last remaining kakapo in the wild? Could there be South Island kokako lurking here somewhere?

The land around West Cape, New Zealand's western extremity, is the remotest part of the mainland – the last frontier. Getting there is the overlander's 'summit' – the horizontal equivalent of a soaring, difficult and seldom-climbed peak. Only a handful of experienced trampers and scientists ever traverse on foot the region between Dusky Sound and Chalky Inlets. They re-

Left: *Puysegur Point marks the southern entrance of Preservation Inlet – a bleak site climatically, but it supports a rich shrubland and grassland. It has mainland New Zealand's remotest lighthouse .*
Lou Sanson

Above: *West Cape, New Zealand's western extremity. Woodland vegetation surrounding an outcrop of granite. The main trees in this mosaic are manuka, mountain beech, rata and pink pine.*
Alan Mark

Silver beech forest dominates the landscape in this view south-west from Borland Saddle. Island Lake, formed by an old landslip, is partly visible.
Peter Johnson

quire a heightened sense of adventure, extreme fitness, a tolerance of wet feet and the patience to sit out floods on scanty rations.

The Wilmot Pass and Borland Saddle roads offer the closest approach by vehicle to West Cape. From either road, the Cape is 75km away, and that is in a straight line, of which there are very few in Fiordland. Walking tracks penetrate only a fraction of the region. West Cape is 50km from the nearest tracks (Dusky and south coast).

Around the coast from Dusky Sound (which is at the same latitude as Dunedin, 45 degrees 45 minutes south) to Te Waewae Bay the landscape is one of relatively low relief, and there is a pattern of hills sloping down to meet the sea with 50m-high cliffs. The land is cut by numerous rivers, many of them fed by lakes occupying old glacial cirques.

The South is wet. Precipitation at the coast is probably in the order of 1,600-2,000mm, rising to 4,000-5000mm in the moun-

Right: *Lake Hauroko, deepest New Zealand lake (462m), is sheer-sided in places.*
Peter Johnson

Below: *A 10-day-old chick of mottled petrel* Pterodroma inexpecta *in a burrow on a small island in Lake Hauroko. The island, some 20km from the sea, supports a colony of about 120 pairs – the species' only known inland colony. Most mottled petrels breed on islands off Stewart Island or in the fiords, or at The Snares. Wintering in the North Pacific, the birds return in October to breed. Their daily pattern is to arrive at the colony after dusk and depart for feeding grounds at sea before dawn – 4am in mid-summer. Burrows are dug in the peat layer under rata-kamahi forest and both parents feed the single chick. Mottled petrels, which are frosty grey and roughly the size of rock pigeons but slimmer, were known to Maori as korure and their chicks taken as muttonbirds. Weka are thought to predate eggs and perhaps chicks, though an intruder in a mottled petrel burrow may be deterred by a stream of stomach oil spat out by the chick.*
Wynston Cooper

tains. The South may have more rain days than the North and is probably cloudier. Fogs are prevalent along the coastal belt. It is also a windy region, bearing the brunt of the south-westerly airstreams. Average windspeed at Puysegur Point has been calculated at 34kph, which makes it New Zealand's windiest spot.

Contributing to the South's moist image are hundreds of lakes and tarns, which occur at just about any altitude. In the far south are a series of lakes that are separated from the Waiau catchment and drain independently to the sea. Two of these, Lakes Hauroko and Poteriteri, are large, long and narrow.

Hauroko, 157m above sea level, has an area of 68 sq km, a long axis of 33.7km with a maximum width of 7.8km. It is New Zealand's deepest lake. A maximum depth of 462m has been recorded at about the midway point of the main axis, west of Mary Island. Hauroko, which means 'soughing or moaning of the wind', is notorious for its northerly gales. The lake can be a millpond one minute and a hazardous experience for small boats the next, as a fresh northerly springs out of nowhere and kicks up steep breaking waves.

To the west and roughly parallel with Hauroko is Lake Poteriteri, 42.5 sq km in area, 27km long and just 3km in maximum width, which makes it spectacularly narrow. The lake runs virtually north-south and its southern end is connected to the sea, only 8km away, by the Waitutu River.

Further west are the small lakes of Hakapoua and Kiwi, which are drained by Big River and Kiwi Burn respectively. Back in the Cameron Mountains, some 22km due north of Big River mouth, is Lake Monk, 582m above sea level, with an area of 1.2 sq km, a long axis of 2.3km and a maximum depth of 100m.

The region's southern extremity is the rocky coastline of Waitutu, an area renowned for its uplifted marine terraces and its rich forest cover.

BEECH AND PODOCARP FORESTS

Silver beech *Nothofagus menziesii* is the most widespread tall tree in Fiordland. It is more tolerant of wet sites and leached soils than either of the two other beech species found there – mountain beech *N. solandri* var. *cliffortioides* and red beech *N. fusca* – or any of the large trees in the podocarp family, such as rimu, kahikatea, totara, miro and matai.

Pure stands of silver beech – known as tawhai to Maori – are common in the south-west, and almost everywhere it forms the treeline, which is generally about 850-1,000m above sea level. Treeline silver beech are stunted, gnarled and of uniform height (up to 10m but often less), and the branches are typically draped with the pale-green *Usnea* lichen known as old man's beard, as at Borland Saddle and on the Kepler Track.

The bark of silver beech is distinctively white or silvery, especially in young trees. The tree's toothed leaves are intermediate in size between red beech leaves, which are larger, softer and paler, and the small smooth-edged leaves of mountain beech.

Silver beech reaches about 25m in height and will compete for canopy space with podocarp trees. On steeper sites with thin wet and perhaps podzolised soils, yellow-silver pine *Lepidothamnus intermedius* shows out as yellowish dabs on the dark canvas of beech. A medium-sized podocarp but one of the hardiest, it reaches a height of about 12m.

Where the soils are deeper and more fertile – at the head of fiords, for example, or near rivers and lakes – the larger podocarps are usually emergent above the beech. Rimu *Dacrydium cupressinum*, unmistakable with its drooping olive-green foliage, can reach a height of over 40m. There are some

Above: *The native mistletoe* Alepis flavida, *rarer in Fiordland than the red-flowered species, produces yellow flowers that turn to orange. Mistletoes – parasitic shrubs – provide a dramatic splash of colour in lowland forest when they flower in summer. Scarlet-flowered* Peraxilla colensoi *is the commonest, reaching 3m across. It is usually found on silver beech.* P. tetrapetala, *which also has red flowers, is more likely on mountain beech.*
Chris Rance

Below: *Lichen city. This small section of the trunk of a silver beech tree above Borland Saddle is host to at least six lichen species.* Usnea capillacea, *old man's beard, is easily recognisable dangling from the tree. At centre is the blue-green* Psoroma leprolomum. *Patches of yellow-green* Pseudocyphellaria coronata *lie above it. Other species include apple-green* Nephroma australe *on the upper side of the trunk below the* Psoroma.
Neville Peat

Above: *'Pixie cups'. A common species of lichen in the genus* Cladonia *produces bright-red spore-bearing rims (apothecia) on its little cups, as in this example from Borland Saddle.*
Peter Johnson

impressive specimens around Lake Manapouri, notably at Stockyard Cove. Of lesser stature but prominent all the same in mixed lowland forest are Hall's totara *Podocarpus hallii* and miro *Prumnopitys ferruginea*. The latter's 20mm-long purple-red drupes (reflected in the genus name, which means 'plum fruit') are favourite food of New Zealand pigeon, which is large enough to consume the drupes whole.

Understorey trees include mountain toatoa *Phyllocladus alpinus*, lancewood *Pseudopanax crassifolius*, haumakaroa *P. simplex*, mapou *Myrsine australis*, *M. divaricata*, rohutu *Neomyrtus pedunculata*, broadleaf *Griselinia littoralis*, leatherwood *Olearia colensoi*, hupiro *Coprosma foetidissima* and the tree fern wheki *Dicksonia squarrosa*. In the west, the rata-kamahi association becomes prominent.

The understorey in beech forest is rather more open than in podocarp, where shrubs are more prolific and supplejack vines entangle everything. The crown fern piupiu *Blechnum discolor* is often dominant on the floor of beech forests.

The lowland forest on the south coast – Waitutu forest – is special in a number of ways, not the least being that it survives on a flight of marine terraces that might have been cleared for farming or settlement if roads had ever been built into the area.

Rimu is the tallest tree (up to an altitude of about 300m) and abundant. Miro is sometimes co-dominant. On the lower terraces (below 300m), rimu is mixed with Hall's totara, rata, kamahi and silver beech. Mountain beech tends to replace silver beech above 300m, and on wetter sites the podocarps yellow-silver pine *Lepidothamnus intermedius* and pink pine *Halocarpus biformis* are emergent. Both species are mixed with manuka *Leptospermum scoparium* and mingimingi *Cyathodes juniperina* on boggy sites.

Below: *The short-jawed* Galaxias postvectis, *which grows to about 25cm, is rarely seen and is considered a threatened species. In Fiordland, it is known only from some southern rivers and streams.*
G.A. Eldon

Above: *South coast. The marine terraces of Waitutu support the largest coastal flatlands left in New Zealand with vegetation intact. And here in Waitutu forest is the richest assemblage of podocarp trees in Fiordland. The mouth of the Wairaurahiri River, which drains Lake Hauroko, appears at bottom right. It is an important river for native fish. Four migratory galaxiids have been recorded in the Wairaurahiri – giant kokopu, banded kokopu, koaro and short-jawed kokopu (see page 38).*
Alan Mark

Above: *Rising to 1067m, the summit crest of The Hump is east of Waitutu and south of Lake Hauroko. It is studded with sandstone tors. It has a distinctive flora, including the local endemic* Pimelea crosby-smithiana, *a neat small shrub (up to 40cm tall) with white flowers grading to a rose colour. It also occurs on adjacent mountains. Other distinctive shrubs are* Olearia crosby-smithiana *and* Hebe canterburiensis. *The nearest populations of the latter are on the West Coast. Another low-alpine shrub occurring on The Hump is* Parahebe brevistylus, *which favours streamsides. It occurs as far north as Franz Josef.*

Ian Turnbull

Left: *Swamp forest near the Lake Hauroko outlet of the Wairaurahiri River, featuring kahikatea* Dacrycarpus dacryioides. *This podocarp, the tallest of the family in New Zealand, prefers fertile soils, as on river flats. It will tolerate wet conditions but may not reach its potential height (60m) and girth.*

Peter Johnson

Above: *Clouds of flowers almost obscure the narrow leaves of the daisy* Olearia crosby-smithiana, *a Fiordland endemic shrub, growing to about 3m in height. Pictured here with* Dracophyllum menziesii, *it is found on southern Fiordland mountains, including The Hump.*

Chris Ward

Willowherb

Glossy green leaves and impressed veins characterise a willowherb *Epilobium matthewsii* that is widespread in Fiordland and endemic to the region except for one Stewart Island (Tin Range) record. It grows from sea level to 900m at wet sites such as waterfalls and moist banks and rocks.

The dwarf buttercup Ranunculus acaulis, a common coastal plant seen here on the Coal River iron sands near Breaksea Sound, has solitary flowers that are rather large compared to its glossy ternate (arranged in threes) leaves.
Peter Johnson

Shrubland

The largest population of the nationally rare shrub *Pittosporum obcordatum* occurs in Back Valley south of Lake Manapouri's Hope Arm, where it was discovered in 1981. The small-leaved species, which has sweetly-scented yellow flowers and separate male and female plants, is associated with shrubland areas in lowland forest, where it reaches 5m in height. It has a divaricating habit and at Back Valley it forms impenetrable thickets. There are only a few small populations in the North Island and two records from the Catlins area.

Small shrubs of the genus *Leonohebe* are distinctive throughout Fiordland, but especially so in the south. The closely branched 20cm-high *L. pauciflora*, a Fiordland endemic, is found south of the Murchison Mountains. The slender whipcord *L. laingii* grows only in alpine areas of southwest Fiordland and on Stewart Island, while the larger *L. hectorii* replaces it further north and east. The central Fiordland endemic *L. petriei murrellii* grows on Mt Burns, whereas *L. petriei* extends into the Livingstone and Takitimu Mountains.

The speargrass Aciphylla congesta, here flowering on Mt Burns above the Borland Saddle, ranges as high as 2,000m. It occurs in fellfield and is often growing amongst snow-patch grass Chionochloa oreophila.
Rory Logan

Celmisia inaccessa, *one of five daisy species in the genus* Celmisia *that is endemic to Fiordland, is restricted to moist, shady bluffs and debris in the limestone country of central Fiordland. It grows to about 1,100m above sea level. The flowerhead is about 40mm across. C. inaccessa and another mountain daisy,* C. praestans *have restricted ranges in Fiordland, with the latter occurring in subalpine herbfield at the head of Long Sound (Preservation Inlet).*

Rory Logan

Celmisia traversii, *pictured here on Mt Luxmore, is a distinctive mountain daisy, with a disjunct distribution (northwest Nelson and Fiordland). It is a feature of low-alpine areas of southern Fiordland, standing out in snow grass/herbfield habitats because of its tomentum, which is a rich velvety rusty-brown, its dark-purple midrib and reddish-brown flower stalks. The flower is up to 60mm across.*

Neville Peat

The speargrass Aciphylla crosby-smithii, *pictured here on Mt Burns above Borland Saddle, is best represented in southern Fiordland. It occurs in the alpine zone to about 1,600m, forming cushions up to 60cm across.*

Rory Logan

The buttercup Ranunculus buchananii, *pictured here on Mt Burns, is one of the high-alpine zone's most spectacular flowering plants. An inhabitant of southern South Island mountains, it grows to an altitude of about 2,400m.*

Neill Simpson

Tussocks of Chionochloa spiralis *sprout from limestone bluffs in Takahe Valley, Murchison Mountains, at an altitude of about 950m. The species appears to be restricted to limestone sites in Fiordland. Palatable to deer, it has a scattered distribution. The first specimen was collected in Takahe Valley in 1955; the next from Monk Lake Valley in 1960. In 1989, several plants were identified at the entrance to limestone caves below Mt Luxmore. C. spiralis is named for the characteristic spiral curling of its dry old leaf sheaths. Its leaves, less than 1m long, and seeds contain high concentrations of calcium which it acquires from the limestone. It is often found with an* undescribed Hebe *that is also endemic to Fiordland and occurs on limestone.*
Kelvin Lloyd

SNOW-GRASS COMMUNITIES

Fiordland, including the Livingstone and Takitimu Mountains and Longwood Range, is a showcase region for the genus *Chionochloa*, the snow grasses or tussocks.

In New Zealand, there are 22 *Chionochloa* species (33 if you count subspecies) – all of them endemic. Fourteen species or subspecies are found in the wider Fiordland region. Three species occur only in Fiordland – *C. spiralis*, *C. ovata*, and needle-tipped *C. acicularis*. *C. ovata*, highly palatable to deer, occurs on alpine bluffs (to 1,400m) in western Fiordland. Deer have restricted its distribution in the past but with the reduction in deer numbers, this species is recovering. *C. spiralis* also has a restricted distribution – limestone country in the Murchison, Kepler and Cameron Mountains. *C. acicularis*, which is found in the southwest south of Cascade Saddle from lowland sites to 1,200m above sea level, is not palatable to deer.

Most non-forested habitats are occupied by one or more of the snow grasses, from frosty valley floors to the high-alpine zone. Some species like permanently damp sites (for example *C. ovata*), others prefer the well-drained areas (*C. pallens*). *Chionochloa* (meaning 'snow grass' in Greek) provide habitat for a diverse collection of subshrubs, herbs and cushion plants, not to mention invertebrate communities.

The genus has undergone considerable revision recently, which has given rise to a suite of subspecies. For example, *C. rigida amara* (formerly *C. flavescens*) generally occurs west of the main divide, with *C. r. rigida* found in the east.

Chionochloa teretifolia, *unpalatable to deer, is confined to the low-alpine zone of southern Fiordland and the Longwood Range. The rounded leaves carry a distinctive pattern of tiny hairs, which glisten with water droplets after a heavy dew or light rain.*
Peter Johnson

SOUTHERN INVERTEBRATES

A rainforest, even at Fiordland's temperate latitudes, supports invertebrate animals in abundance. The forest floor, covered in leaf mould, mosses and lichens, is alive with beetles, worms, snails, mites, springtails and spiders. Fiordland south of the Hunter Mountains contains numerous species not found anywhere else.

Extensive boggy areas in the west and south support a relatively small but distinctive invertebrate fauna, exemplified by the elegant diurnal moth *Aponotoreas synclinalis*, a geometrid whose larvae feed on wire rush *Empodisma minus*. Adjoining drier habitats are often richer. For example, 45 species of land-snail were found in a brief survey in Waitutu forest.

Higher up, the shrublands and grasslands abound with alpine invertebrates, many of them first described from the Hunter Mountains, Cleughearn Peak near Lake Monowai or The Hump – the focus of early entomological forays. Typically, this fauna combines a dazzling array of brightly-coloured diurnal species with a slightly more sombre nocturnal variety.

Among the diurnal ones are several giant weevil species, including *Lyperobius coxalis*, plus a flightless chafer beetle *Prodontria setosa*, and several moths, including *Proteodes clarkei* and *Notoreas* new species, all endemic to the south. A large brown-and-white striped diurnal moth *Aponotoreas villosa* is found only in the mountains of southern Fiordland and on the Longwood Range. The short-winged (brachypterous) female calls to attract males from on top of snow grasses (*Chionochloa*), the larval food plant – a unique form of behaviour for its genus.

Colourful diurnal totricid moths related to leaf-rollers are an important element of the moth fauna of Fiordland. Mostly reliant on shrubs of *Cassinia*, *Leonohebe* or *Hebe* as larval hosts, this group includes *Pyrgotis consentiens*, *Planotortrix flammea*, *Harmologa sanguinea* and *H. festiva*, which is restricted to southern Fiordland.

Above: *This small moth of the genus* Notoreas, *with a wingspan of 18mm, flies by day over high-alpine cushionfield contain-ing the larval food plant* Kelleria croizatii. *The species, yet to be formally described, is found only in southern Fiordland, the Takitimu Mountains and Mt Anglem, Stewart Island.*

Brian Patrick

Above: *The short-horned grasshopper* Alpinacris tumidicauda (*length up to 25mm*) *lives in the drier eastern mountains. It is characterised by a white strip behind its head and an orange posterior. Short-horned grasshoppers* (Acrididae) *are not a feature of Fiordland grasslands except in eastern mountains such as the Hunter, Kepler and Murchison Mountains. Three species are found there –* Sigaus australis, S. obelisci *and the one pictured.*

Brian Patrick

The Fiordland snow grasses, *Chionochloa*
C. acicularis endemic, Fiordland National Park
C. conspicua western and southern South Island
C. crassiuscula directa Hunter, Takitimu, Longwood
C. crassiuscula torta Fiordland National Park and Longwood
C. macra eastern Fiordland, Takitimu, Livingstone
C. oreophila main divide
C. ovata endemic, western Fiordland
C. pallens cadens Takitimu, Longwood, southwest South Island
C. rubra cuprea southern South Island
C. rigida Livingstone, Takitimu, eastern South Island
C. rigida amara Fiordland, Stewart Island, Longwood, West Coast
C. spiralis endemic, Fiordland National Park
C. teretifolia southern Fiordland, Longwood
C. vireta southwest South Island

Impressive if slow-moving, the stag beetle Geodorcus helmsi *(length, up to 35mm), seen here crawling over moss on Hawea Island, Breaksea Sound, is one of two large species of flightless stag beetles occurring in south-west Fiordland. This species is found in coastal grasslands and also in forest by day, where it is abundant. A related species* G. philpotti, *is restricted to The Hump-Waitutu forests. Both have larvae that live on and within rotten logs.*
Peter Johnson

This undescribed depressariid moth of the genus Proteodes *(wingspan 25mm) has been recorded only in Waitutu so far. Its larvae feed on the hard-leaved shrub mingimingi* Cyathodes juniperina. *Fiordland is renowned for its* Proteodes *moths. Three species are endemic to the region –* P. clarkei, *which is found in the high-alpine zone of the Hunter Mountains and has a short-winged flightless female;* P. smithi, *widespread at the treeline; and the species pictured. Another species,* P. carnifex, *defoliates mountain beech (page 34).*
Brian Patrick

The caddis Philorheithrus lacustris *(wingspan 35mm) is widespread in Fiordland to about 1,000m above sea level. The larvae inhabit a case and live in fast-flowing streams. Caddis, a sister group to the moths, have hairs instead of scales. The larvae are invariably aquatic. So far, 84 caddis species have been recorded in the wider Fiordland area, with only one,* Tiphobiosis salmoni, *being endemic. Several other species, although not restricted to Fiordland, are best known from there, including the black* Psilochorema embersoni, Edpercivalia harrisoni *and the large* Costachorema hebdomon.
Brian Patrick

Above: *This large bear weevil* Rhynchodes ursus *(length over 25mm) can fly but is mostly encountered walking on tree trunks in beech forest. The weevil family of beetles (Curculionidae) is the most species-rich group of fauna existing on the planet today. An estimated one in five species on earth is a weevil.*
Brian Patrick

Left: *The chunky weevil* Anagotus oconnori *(length 18mm), collected at 1,300m in the Murchison Mountains. The notched leaves of the lily* Astelia nivicola *are a giveaway sign that this weevil is hidden nearby.*
Brian Patrick

Stoners

Fiordland is one of the main centres of diversity in New Zealand for the aquatic group of insects known as stoners (stoneflies), even though there have been only superficial studies of them to date and more species will no doubt come to light.

Eleven species are confined to Fiordland or discrete areas within the region. Most are flightless, having either no wings (apterous) or short wings (brachypterous).

The giant stoner Holcoperla angularis (length 25mm) live in wet rocky areas in the alpine zone. The adults are active by day – an amazing sight as they crawl over damp granite rocks above 1,400m.
Brian Patrick

Fiordland's stoners	
Apteryoperla illiesi	Homer area (apterous)
A. monticola	Doubtful Sound area (apterous)
A. ramsayi	Wilmot Pass (apterous)
A. tillyardi	Hamley Peak (apterous)
Christaperla eylesi	Fiordland, widespread (winged)
Holcoperla angularis	Fiordland, widespread (apterous)
Notonemoura spinosa	Wilmot Pass (winged)
Zelandoperla denticulata	Fiordland, widespread (winged)
Zelandobius brevicauda	Turret Range (brachypterous)
Z. dugdalei	Darran Mountains (winged)
Vesicaperla dugdalei	Fiordland, widespread (apterous)

FOREST BIRDS

Although introduced predators and browsing animals have had an impact on Fiordland's native forest birds, the region remains a stronghold for a number of threatened species, among them South Island kaka, yellow-crowned parakeet, South Island robin, New Zealand falcon and yellowhead (page 00).

South Island kaka *Nestor meridionalis*, larger than its North Island cousin and distinguished from the latter by a more prominent white or grey crown, is fairly evenly distributed through Fiordland lowland forest, although numbers are highest along the south coast. They are frequently encountered along the shores of Lakes Te Anau, Manapouri and Monowai and around Dusky Sound (there is a record from Cooper Island, Dusky Sound, in autumn 1975 of a flock of 50 kaka feeding on rimu fruit). In the 1890s, goldminers at Preservation Inlet shot kaka for food.

In the same genus as kea but rarely seen above the treeline, kaka feed on nectar and podocarp fruit in summer/autumn and invertebrates through much of the year. They are highly mobile and move seasonally for food. They rely on old or rotting trees for insect larvae and holes to nest in.

A smaller member of the parrot family, yellow-crowned parakeet or kakariki *Cyanoramphus auriceps* is found mainly in eastern Fiordland beech forests. Often seen associating with yellowheads, kakariki, like the yellowhead and kaka, depend on extensive tracts of mature forest for survival. At nesting, they utilise holes in trees, living or dead. For some decades there has been debate over whether the orange-fronted parakeet is a separate species (named *C. malherbi* last century) or simply an interbreeding colour morph of the yellow-crowned. There are only very small numbers of orange-fronted parakeet in Fiordland.

Both the yellow-crowned and red-crowned parakeet *C. novaeseelandiae* were found together in some parts of Fiordland (for example, Hollyford Valley and Murchison Mountains) in the past, but since late last century the red-crowned parakeet has declined and is now an extremely rare species on the Fiordland mainland.

Fiordland has a reasonably full range of the more common South Island forest birds, including bellbird, tui, New Zealand pigeon, South Island fantail, South Island robin, South Island tomtit, brown creeper, grey warbler, silvereye and, smallest of them all, South Island rifleman.

A member of the wren family, South Island rifleman or titipounamu *Acanthisitta chloris* is widespread in Fiordland and seems to prosper from the beech 'mast' seasons, when it can be the most numerous bird in the forest. Always busy and mercurial, rifleman are fond of hopping up and down trunks and along branches in pursuit of insects. They are commonly seen in

On the brink

South Island kokako *Callaeas cinerea*, an orange-wattled forest bird closely related to the blue-wattled North Island kokako, is on the brink of extinction. Sightings or signs are reported only sporadically from remote forested areas, including Fiordland. At Christmas 1994, a kokako-like call – a series of deep resonant organ notes – was heard by a couple boating on Lake Monowai near Eel Creek. The report added to the evidence of a remnant kokako population in the area between Lake Hauroko and the Grebe Valley. Through the 1980s there were several sightings or calls reported.

In 1967 feathers of kokako were found in a rat trap at Borland Saddle, and, earlier, in the 1940s, there were several sightings of a bird answering the kokako's description – a bulky blue-grey bird, larger than a tui – from the Electric River area west of Monowai. The only other signi-ficant report came from Poison Bay on the northern coast of Fiordland. A New Zealand Forest Service expedition reported seeing a kokako flying near the river mouth in October 1975. Its orange wattles were identified while it was perched in a tree for a short time. But a Wildlife Service team found no sign of kokako in the Poison Bay area when the report was investigated.

Left: *South Island robin or toutouwai*
Petroica australis, *like the fantail, will
approach humans within the forest in
the hope they have stirred up some
insect food. Whereas fantails usually
stay above ground level, robins are
often seen scuffing up the forest litter
or hopping around fallen trees. This
habit makes them vulnerable to stoats.
They occur mainly in eastern areas of
Fiordland. In the west, robins are rare.
Populations seem scattered, with
Breaksea Island, despite its history of
rats, holding one of the largest western
populations.*

Ian Southey

groups. Their call is a repetitive high-pitched 'tsit-tsit'.

Bellbird or makomako *Anthornis melanura* are also abundant in parts of Fiordland, especially where podocarps are mixed with the beech, as in Waitutu. Tui, which are also nectar feeders, are not as numerous in Fiordland but are widely distributed. They are attracted to forest rich in the large podocarps, which occurs only in pockets. Back Valley south of Lake Manapouri is one such place. Tui are found in small numbers only in beech forest.

One of the most charming of the bush birds is brown creeper or pipipi *Mohoua novaeseelandiae*, a South Island endemic, which shares the same genus as yellowhead. Brown creeper are typically encountered in flocks flitting through the canopy, trilling melodiously.

Kakapo – Lost parrot?

Kakapo *Strigops habroptilis* has probably disappeared altogether from Fiordland. Nocturnal and all but flightless, the world's heaviest parrot (up to 3.5kg) is now confined to island refuges and is critically endangered. Fiordland and Stewart Island were its last mainland refuges, and as numbers plummeted through the impact of stoats, rats and wild cats, kakapo were progressively transferred to safe islands. Two males caught in Sinbad Gully and Poseidon Valley south of Milford Sound in 1981, and flown to Maud Island in the Marlborough Sounds, were the last to be transferred out of Fiordland.

There has been no positive evidence of kakapo in Fiordland since 1987, but sightings and sign are occasionally reported. In 1894-1900, conservationist Richard Henry transferred 350 to 400 kakapo on to predator-free islands, mainly in Dusky Sound, but all these populations have died out. Stoats were able to swim to the islands.

DOC

A blue duck resting by the Lyvia River at the head of Doubtful Sound.

Ian Southey

WATER BIRDS

A water world like Fiordland provides habitats for a many different aquatic birds. Some of them, like New Zealand scaup, grey duck, paradise shelduck and New Zealand shoveler, are common and not considered to be at risk; a few freshwater species, however, are vulnerable or endangered because of the impact of predators, stoats in particular . . .

A pair of brown teal photographed at Gair Loch.

Ian Southey

Blue duck

Blue duck *Hymenolaimus malacorhynchos*, a threatened species, is rather secretive, although it is not a conspicuous bird because of its territorial nature and its use of bouldery fast-flowing mountain streams off the beaten track. The slate-blue colour, with spotted chestnut breast feathers, makes an excellent camouflage.

The ducks, active at night as well as during daylight hours, feed on aquatic insects and crustaceans, which they scrape from rocks with their specially adapted bill. Large webbed feet aid their ability to manoeuvre in swift rivers. In deep water they will dive and stay submerged for up to about 20 seconds.

Usually blue ducks nest near water under logs or clumps of vegetation or around rocks; up to nine eggs are laid and incubated by the female. They fight viciously to defend their territory, using a spur on their wings as a weapon. Their Maori name, whio, echoes the wheezy whistle of the male. Both sexes look alike.

Brown teal

Brown teal *Anas aucklandica chlorotis* is seriously endangered. Once widespread in lowland swamps, swamp forest and quiet backwaters throughout New Zealand, the species is represented in the South Island only by a small and declining population in Fiordland. Probably the best place to see them – singly or in pairs, for the days when they could be seen in flocks have gone – is in the Seaforth catchment (Dusky Track).

Brown teal are aggressively territorial. They usually nest in grass or sedges near water and lay 4-8 eggs. They feed mainly at night on insects, insect larvae, worms, snails and succulent foliage.

Stewart Island lost its brown teal to cat predation by 1972. Stoats and their small population size are the main threats to their survival in Fiordland. In the North Island, there are remnant populations in Northland, Great Barrier Island and Little Barrier Island. The Fiordland birds appear to have a richer colour all over, but especially on the breast, than their Northland counterparts.

ENDEMIC DOLPHIN

Perhaps the last word on Fiordland's southern region should go to Hector's dolphin *Cephalorhynchus hectori*, the world's smallest dolphin and one of the rarest. A population of 300-400 is resident in Te Waewae Bay.

Only about 1.4m long, with a rounded dorsal fin, rounded flippers, pale colouring (mainly light grey to white) and no beak, Hector's dolphins are readily identified. They do not leap out of the water as often as dusky dolphins and they tend to keep fairly close to shore.

Hector's dolphins seem to remain within their home ranges and have little or no contact with other populations. The populations nearest to Te Waewae Bay are at Porpoise Bay (Catlins) and Jackson Bay (West Coast). The fiords appear to be a 'no-go' zone for them. Genetic studies suggest the populations on the east and west coasts of the South Island have been isolated from each other for thousands of years.

The species is New Zealand's only endemic cetacean (whales, dolphins and porpoises).

Below: *Hector's dolphin mother and calf.*
Steve Dawson

TAKITIMU AND LONGWOOD
Adjacent ranges

Forming the high ground east of the lower Waiau River, and dominating the skyline from the Southland Plains, are two mountain blocks – the Takitimu Mountains and Longwood Range. Although they are basically of the same geological origin (volcanism dating back over 250 million years), these two mountain masses are quite different in character. The Takitimu Mountains stand tall, steep, saw-toothed and deeply incised, with extensive rock screes thwarting the establishment of vegetation on the steeper slopes. Spence Peak, 1,654m, is the high point.

Maori see the arching prominence of the Takitimu Mountains as the petrified remains of the ancestral canoe, Takitimu. The Longwoods, on the other hand, are more rounded and sprawling, wholly covered in forest, shrubland or grassland, and half the height. It is possible to drive to the summit crest of the Longwood Range (Bald Hill, 804m).

Products of the volcanism are more visible in the Takitimu Mountains – red and green breccia, andesite tuffs, basalt sills and pillow lavas. Formed as a result of volcanic eruptions under the sea, the distinctive pillow lavas occur in fine-grained marine sediments and show out clearly on cliffs in the Gibraltar Burn at the southern end of the range. The impact of glaciation in the last two million years is evident in the Takitimu Mountains, where there are U-shaped valleys, cirques and moraines. Active scree and talus slopes give these mountains a character distinct from the ranges in Fiordland National Park – a character more in keeping with the erosion-prone Canterbury mountains. At the upper margins of the screes are curious landscape features – stone stripes, polygons and stone terraces.

As the eastern boundary riders of Fiordland, the two ranges share some of the special fauna and flora of the main part of Fiordland, as well as supporting a distinct suite of species.

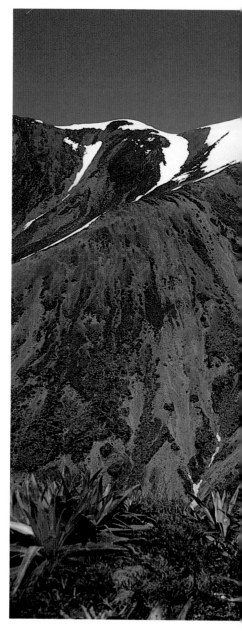

Left: Hebe crawii, *a rare low shrub, is found in scree or fellfield in the Takitimu Mountains. The species has a restricted distribution that includes the Eyre, Garvie and Umbrella Mountains.*
Chris Rance

Above: *Scree slopes on Clare Peak (1,490m), Takitimu Mountains. Alpine plants in the foreground include* Dracophyllum uniflorum *(reddish shrub) and the stiff-leaved grey daisy* Celmisia semicordata *var* stricta.
Chris Rance

TAKITIMU VEGETATION

In the Takitimu Mountains, the steep scree slopes, restricted snowbank areas and dry low-alpine shrubland zone support plant communities somewhat different from the mountains to the west, in Fiordland National Park.

Scree chickweed *Stellaria roughii* and the handsome daisy *Haastia sinclairii* are both extremely well camouflaged in the scree setting. The local endemic *Parahebe* new species and edelweiss *Leucogenes grandiceps* occupy rocky ridges while the compact, creeping willow herb *Epilobium tasmanicum* and green cushions of *Phyllachne colensoi* are typical of fellfield areas. Curiously, *E. tasmanicum* is common in the Takitimu and Livingstone Mountains and various Otago mountains, and is shared with Tasmania and the Kosciusko mountains of Australia, but does not occur in Fiordland National Park.

Grasslands of slim snow tussock *Chionochloa macra* contain scattered shrubs of *Leonohebe hectorii* and cushions of *Kelleria croizatii* and *Colobanthus buchananii*. At lower altitudes, the grasslands of *Chionochloa pallens cadens* and *C. rigida* are distinctive for the presence of silver daisy *Celmisia semicordata* var *stricta* and smaller herbs such as *Aciphylla lyallii*, *Gingidia decipiens* and *Celmisia densiflora*.

Above: *Alpine shrubland and grassland in a tributary of the Spence Burn, Takitimu Mountains. The grey shrub is* Olearia moschata, *which is growing amongst* Leonohebe mooreae.
Chris Rance

Right: *The scree weta* Deinacrida connectens *(length up to 50mm) has a striking pattern of stripes along its abdomen and reddish margins to its thorax. This specimen is a female from Spence Peak.*
George Gibbs

Far right: *The hairy alpine grasshopper* Sigaus obelisci *(length 35mm) is common on the Takitimu Mountains in both scree and fellfield habitats. Larvae and adults are both herbivores. They play a fundamental role in determining the structure of plant communities by their differential feeding behaviour.*
Brian Patrick

Torrentfish *Cheimarrichthys fosteri* has been recorded in Redcliff Creek, a tributary of the lower Waiau River. As its name suggests, this native fish is at home in 'white water'. Distributed widely though rarely seen, it may be lurking under boulders in rapids. It grows to about 16cm in length. Like the galaxiids of the whitebait group, it spends its juvenile months at sea following spawning and returns to the rivers in spring.

Another freshwater native fish that lives in the Takitimu Mountains is the upland bully *Gobiomorphus breviceps*, a stocky eastern South Island species that grows to a length of 10cm. It carries orange spots on its head. A non-migratory alpine galaxiid, *Galaxias paucispondylus,* is found in the headwaters of the Oreti River in the Thomson Mountains east of Lake North Mavora.

Giant kokopu *Galaxias argenteus* have been recorded at Lake George, which lies close to the sea at the southern end of the Longwood Range. Their presence testifies to the intact nature of the 2km-long lake, which is regarded as the only coastal wetland of its kind in Southland still in natural condition. Its water and shores provide habitat for waterfowl, fernbird and marsh crake.

The shrubland zone is dominated in places by turpentine shrub *Dracophyllum uniflorum*, *Leonohebe odora* and snow totara *Podocarpus nivalis*. The herbs *Celmisia petriei* or *Ourisia caespitosa* are also prevalent in places. A taller, more dense shrubland occurs lower down, featuring inaka *Dracophyllum longifolium*, *Cassinia vauvilliersii* and *Olearia nummulariifolia*. It becomes impenetrable when joined by the large speargrass *Aciphylla horrida* and the shrubs *Olearia bullata* and *Aristotelia fruticosa*. Other shrub species of note on the range are an endemic *Hebe* that is similar to *H. rakaiensis*, *Leonohebe annulata*, which is known elsewhere only on the rock faces of the St Mary's Range in North Otago, and *Hebe haastii* var *humilis*, which grows in rocky areas of northern Fiordland.

TAKITIMU INVERTEBRATES

The screes of the Takitimu Mountains are home to the stout grasshopper *Sigaus obelisci*, black butterfly *Percnodaimon merula*, moth *Tawhitia glaucophanes* and the large scree weta *Deinacrida connectens*. The weta has a disjunct distribution. The nearest known population of *D. connectens* is in western Otago (Rees Saddle area). The species also occurs in high mountains in northwest Otago and through Canterbury.

On the semi-vegetated rocky edges of the screes there are different small animals – for example, a native earwig, an alpine cockroach and a dark-coloured shield bug *Cermatulus nasalis*.

Wetlands harbour a large hepialid moth, *Aoraia aspina*, which flies at dusk or by day when clouds darken the sky, and a pale moth *Asaphodes sericodes*, whose looper larvae feed on various succulent herbs. Numerous carabid beetles and small flies abound in this habitat.

Amongst fellfield, cushionfield is a key habitat for a number of insects, including a large flightless chafer *Scythrodes squalidus*, common in the alpine zone of Central Otago and western areas of Otago, and a small undescribed diurnal moth (*Notoreas* species) that is shared with southern Fiordland. Restricted to the

range is a black-and-white striped giant weevil in the genus *Lyperobius* and yet to be formally described. Larvae and adults are both dependent on herbs of the carrot family.

A medium-sized black cicada *Maoricicada otagoensis macewini* is endemic to the Takitimu Mountains and common in the shrubland zone. Another inhabitant of this zone is the elegant rapid-flying orange ennomid moth *Declana glacialis*, which also lives in main divide areas south to Fiordland. Other day-flying moths include *Dasyuris leucobathra, Asterivora barbigera, Aponotoreas orphnaea, A. insignis* and *A. incompta*.

LONGWOOD VEGETATION

Silver beech dominates all slopes of the Longwood Range up to an abrupt treeline at about 700m. The fairly open understorey features various Coprosma species and an abundance of ferns, lichens and mosses. Conspicuous in the upper forest is the attractive herb *Ourisia crosbyi*, which tends to hug wet banks. Above the forest are two main grassland/shrubland areas – on Bald Hill, the highest point at 804m, and the southern main ridge (764m). A road to a telecommunications facility gives access to the Bald Hill summit.

Two main river systems drain the range – the Waimeamea in the west and Pourakino in the east. The headwaters of both rivers contain an array of low-alpine habitats, flora and fauna. The flora is closely related to that of eastern Fiordland, Stewart Island and the Catlins. A total of 173 vascular plants, 52 mosses and 23 liverworts are known from above the treeline. The absence of speargrasses (*Aciphylla*) is surprising, however.

Above the treeline is a dense shrubland comprising mainly the tree daisy *Olearia nummulariifolia*, mountain toatoa *Phyllocladus alpinus*, pink pine *Halocarpus biformis*, inaka

Below left: The main ridge of the Longwood Range, looking north to Bald Hill (804m) in the distance. Diminutive shrubs and grasses dominate the generally flat tops of the main ridge. A mosaic of wetlands, shrublands, grasslands and diverse herbfields is found above the treeline.
Brian Patrick

Below: The velvetworm or peripatus Ooperipetallus nanus (length 28mm) is confined to the Takitimu Mountains. The egg-laying species has 13 pairs of legs and occurs from the base of the range to 1,300m, inhabiting beech forest, scree and herbfield. The similarly oviparous species, O. viridimaculatus, is widespread in western alpine areas of the South Island including two sites near Lake Te Anau from where it was first described in 1900. Peripatus feed on dead and live prey, spraying a sticky fluid over live prey to subdue them. Nocturnal, they seem to depend on moist habitats under logs or rocks for survival. Peripatus belong to a separate phyllum of invertebrates, Onychophora, which are regarded as the 'missing link' between the segmented worms and the more differentiated and sophisticated arthropods such as insects, spiders and crustaceans. There are at least eight species of the family Peripatopsidae in New Zealand.
Brian Patrick

Dracophyllum longifolium and neatly-rounded shrubs of *Leonohebe odora*.

The shrubland gives way at higher areas to more open grassland and herbfield. Tussocks of *Chionochloa pallens cadens* and *C. teretifolia* form stands that are interspersed with stout shrubs of *Leonohebe mooreae*, *Dracophyllum pearsonii* and *Cassinia vauvilliersii*. Mountain flax *Phormium cookianum* is very common. Pale-green mountain holly *Olearia ilicifolia* is found only on Bald Hill and leatherwood *O. colensoi* occurs only on the main ridge to the south. The large rigid daisy *Celmisia coriacea* is locally common in the grasslands, together with a high diversity of herbs, grasses and sprawling miniature shrubs such as *Kelleria dieffenbachii* and *Leonohebe* aff *odora*. Seven snowgrasses occur on the range.

On the more extensive wetter sites copper tussock *Chionochloa rubra cuprea*, and the curled snow tussocks *C. crassiuscula directa* and *C. crassiuscula torta* are commonly joined by bog-loving cushions of *Donatia novae-zelandiae*, comb sedge *Oreobolus pectinatus*, *Gaimardia setacea* and the moss-like *Centrolepis ciliata*.

The dominant wetland species are wire rush *Empodisma minus*, a moss *Sphagnum australe* and tanglefern *Gleichenia dicarpa* but there are patches where the lily *Astelia linearis*, the daisy *Celmisia glandulosa* and blue-green mats of *Microlaena thomsonii* are prominent. Two shrub podocarps, bog pine *Halocarpus*

Below: *Longwoods beech forest is rich in ferns, with crown fern or piupiu* Blechnum discolor *the dominant ground-cover species.*

Wynston Cooper

bidwillii and pygmy pine *Lepidothamnus laxifolius*, are fairly common in the low-alpine zone, as is the shrub *Leonohebe pauciramosa* and sedge *Carpha alpina*. Seepages support the yellow-flowered daisy *Dolichoglottis lyallii* and a small gentian that was described from the Longwood Range, *Chionogentias lineata*.

LONGWOOD INVERTEBRATES

A surprisingly rich and interesting insect fauna occurs on the low alpine tops of the Longwood Range. Among the five predacious carabid beetles the largest, a regal 40mm or more in length, is named *Mecodema rex*. It is known only from the Longwoods. Of similar length but more robust is the stag beetle *Geodorcus helmsi*. It frequents both forested and non-forested parts of the range. Two grasshoppers *Paprides dugdali* and *Sigaus campestris* jump about the grassland-herbfields on sunny days, while an undescribed cicada (*Kikihia* new species) sings from the shrub-tops.

An intensive study of the moths of the open tops recorded 180 species, among them the large nocturnal hepialids *Aoraia dinodes* and *Heloxycanus patricki*. The related *Dioxycanus fuscus* is crepuscular (dusk-flying). Surprisingly, 29 upland species are also found in non-forest habitats close to Invercargill. The

Right: *Of the eight species of diurnal geometrid moths on the Longwood Range the most striking is* Aponotoreas synclinalis *(wingspan 26mm), which is found in the far south of the South Island and on Stewart Island. The species flies swiftly over wetlands dominated by wire rush, the larval food plant.*
Brian Patrick

Longwood Range invertebrate fauna has its strongest links with Fiordland, with which it shares exclusively the moths *Aponotoreas villosa, Atomotricha prospiciens, Izatha mira, Pseudocoremia berylia* and the tiny diurnal *Glyphipterix aenea*.

Common in the Longwood Range but absent from Fiordland National Park is the handsome snowgrass moth *Orocrambus scutatus*, which is one of four moths described from the range. A distinctive wetlands moth *Scoparia subita* (wingspan 19mm) is common in the Longwood Range, Takitimu Mountains, Fiordland National Park and east to the Slopedown Range in the Catlins.

Linking the range with Stewart Island is an earthworm *Plutellus stewartensi*, which is widespread on the island and occurs also near Orepuki at the south end of the Longwoods. Similarly, the harvestmen *Corinuncia variegata granulata* is known only from the Longwoods and Stewart Island.

Aquatic fauna

The freshwater crayfish *Paranephrops zelandicus* is found commonly in the acidic tarns and streams on the Longwood Range. It shares this habitat with a select group of aquatic insects, including five stoners, two mayflies, five caddis, one red damselfly and New Zealand's only scorpionfly *Nannochorista philpotti*. The shy adult scorpionfly was discovered by Alfred Philpott, an enthusiastic Invercargill entomologist whose early exploration of remote parts of Fiordland and the Longwood Range brought to light many new species. The scorpionfly was formally named in 1917. Later its larvae, up to 17mm long, were found to be feeding on midge larvae in fine organic sediments of pools and quieter parts of streams. Most scorpionfly species around the world have terrestrial larvae.

Left: *Yellow-crowned parakeet or kakariki* Cyanoramphus auriceps, *seen here feeding on mistletoe* Peraxilla colensoi, *are widely distributed in Fiordland and there are populations in the beech forest of the Takitimu Mountains and Longwood Range.*

The yellow-crowned parakeet has a highly varied diet that includes fruit, seeds, flowers and foliage, as well as a range of insects. In the absence of mammalian predators it would probably spend more time on the forest floor.

The brightly-coloured, melodious yellowhead also inhabits the Takitimu and Longwood forests, and kaka have been recorded. These forests support a predictable array of native South Island bush birds, among them New Zealand pigeon, bellbird, tui, brown creeper, South Island robin, South Island fantail, South Island rifleman, South Island tomtit, grey warbler and silvereye.

Ian Southey

Above: *The small stoner* Spaniocerca longicauda *(wingspan 14-19mm) was described from Fiordland and is widespread in southern South Island, including the Longwood Range. It belongs to a family (*Notonemouridae*) of stoners that can leap as well as fly.*
Brian Patrick

MAVORA COUNTRY   Chapter 8
Going east

Mavora country constitutes the north-eastern fringe of Fiordland. Dominant elements are the catchment of the Mararoa River, the South and North Mavora Lakes and the mountains between these waterways and the Eglinton River and Lake Te Anau – specifically, the Livingstone Mountains, Dunton Range, Countess Range and Snowdon Peak.

The Mararoa River is longer than the Waiau into which it drains, but its catchment (44,000 ha) handles only a fraction of the volumes of the Waiau on account of the rainshadow effect of the mountains of Fiordland National Park. Rainfall is as low as 1,600mm in parts of the catchment. The Mararoa's mean flow is estimated at 13 cumecs, although it has achieved 280 cumecs in a big flood. Thus the area is a transition zone, a blend of the open, almost barren landscapes of the Wakatipu region to the north-east and the close-knit, forested character of Fiordland. The climate is cool temperate, with warm summer days producing temperatures in the mid-20s Celsius on the valley floors. At higher altitudes, though, frosts can occur at any time of year, and in winter snow lies for weeks above 1,000m. Strong northwest winds occasionally raise the dust in the Mararoa Valley in spring and summer.

The long and narrow Mavora Lakes, impounded by moraines, occupy upper reaches of the glaciated Mararoa Valley at altitudes of 613 (South) and 619m (North). As elsewhere, the ice

Left: *Steep slopes on the Livingstone Mountains support localised wetlands and a narrow shrubland belt between the beech forest and grassland. North Mavora Lake is at left, linked to South Mavora Lake by a section of the Mararoa River.*

Brian Patrick

Above: *Copper tussock grasslands line the shores of South Mavora Lake, which is overshadowed by the Livingstone Mountains.*

Neville Peat

advanced and retreated to leave glacial features such as U-shaped valleys, outwash terraces, cirques and hanging valleys. The lakes form the centrepiece of the 35,000ha Mavora Lakes Conservation Park. North Mavora is the larger lake, with a length of 11km and a maximum depth of 100m (South Mavora Lake is 2.2km long and up to 30m deep). Both are clear, translucent green and generally lacking in organic matter.

The Livingstone Mountains flank the lakes on their western side, controlled by the Livingstone Fault, which is represented by a prominent escarpment. They embrace a contrasting suite of rock types – volcanic, sedimentary sandstone and ultramafic, with metamorphic greywacke just east of the Mavora 'trough'. The ultramafic (see Chapter 2, page 22) rocks are exposed as remarkable reddish-brown desert-like sequences where plant life has great difficulty establishing.

Mt Richmond (1,674m) is the highest peak in the Livingstone Mountains, but it is topped by Countess Peak (1,829m) in the adjacent and less extensive Countess Range. Snowdon Peak (1,577m) is the high point in a small group of mountains west of the Livingstones that is isolated by the upper reaches and headwaters of the Upukerora and Whitestone Rivers. Both the Countess Range and Snowdon Peak are built of ancient sandstone, Permian to Triassic in age.

Scattered cushion vegetation on a rocky windswept saddle in the Livingstone Mountains. Cushion plants are found in environments of high stress for plants – alpine fellfield and snowbanks, for example, or wetlands, semi-arid habitats and coastal dunes. While most have a taproot, some are mat cushions composed of lateral branches or solid cushions of interconnected rosettes. They typically display an even radial growth form and gently rounded surfaces. Cushion plants have been recorded in 34 families of plants worldwide but the growth form is best developed in New Zealand, Tasmania and Macquarie Island.
Neill Simpson

CONTRASTING PLANT LIFE

The contrast in rock types produces a variety of plant communities above the treeline – substantial grasslands, scattered shrublands and extensive cushionfield and fellfield vegetation at higher altitudes.

The forest, even at the treeline, is predominantly mountain beech on account of the relatively dry conditions, but in places

– notably in Snowdon Forest in the valleys west of the Mavora Lakes – the mountain beech is joined by silver beech and to a lesser extent red beech.

Shrublands consist of the tree daisies *Brachyglottis revolutus, Olearia moschata* and *O. cymbifolia,* in addition to widespread *Dracophyllum* and *Cassinia* species. Above the shrublands lie dense grasslands of *Chionochloa rigida,* often in association with herbs such as *Celmisia semicordata* var *stricta, C. densiflora* and the formidable *Aciphylla horrida.* Scattered shrubs of *Dracophyllum uniflorum* add a red-ochre tinge and mountain toatoa or celery pine *Phyllocladus alpinus* brings a blue-green dimension. The whipcord *Leonohebe hectorii,* snow totara *Podocarpus nivalis* and *Hebe subalpina* are shrub species associated with the grasslands.

Higher still, slim snow tussock *Chionochloa macra* dominates the grasslands and is joined by the daisies *Celmisia hectorii, C. walkeri* and *Brachyglottis bellidioides.* Patches of *Kelleria villosa,* a rush *Marsippospermum gracile, Aciphylla lecomtei* and the small shrub *Hebe buchananii* are locally common.

Cushionfield species include a grey-leaved forget-me-not *Myosotis pulvinaris,* a daphne *Kelleria croizatii, Hectorella caespitosa, Raoulia buchananii* and *Phyllachne colensoi.* The carrot relatives, *Anisotome pilifera* and *A. capillifolia* are locally abundant in rocky areas.

Wetlands are not numerous in these mountains, but where they occur they are likely to feature the comb sedge *Oreobolus pectinatus,* speargrass *Aciphylla pinnatifida,* the bluish *Dracophyllum prostratum,* patches of *Celmisia glandulosa, Kelleria paludosa, Sphagnum* moss, small whipcord-like shrubs of *Leonohebe pauciramosa* and sedges such as *Schoenus pauciflorus.*

The driest and least vegetated parts of these ranges contain a few scree plants such as willowherb *Epilobium porphyrium,* native chickweed *Stellaria roughii* and the daisy *Haastia sinclairii.*

Growing on the ultramafic soils of the Livingstone Mountains and Snowdon Peak are the forget-me-not *Myosotis lyallii,*

the rare willowherb *Epilobium crassum* and the diminutive shrub *Pimelea traversii*. A total of five *Myosotis* species live in the Livingstone Mountains, three of which are undescribed. The ultramafic species has blue-green foliage; the rest are brownish-green. In addition, an undescribed and possibly endemic cress in the genus *Cardamine* grows on the scree. It is a tiny species with simple brown leaves.

Left: Aciphylla horrida *is host to New Zealand's largest noctuid moth* Graphania nullifera *(wingspan 55-80mm). The fat 70mm long, orange and white larvae hatch from eggs often laid in the tall seedheads, moving later to the stalk base and taproot, where they feed in a sticky soup. Sometimes their numbers can kill a plant from feeding pressure. Insects feeding on speargrasses are protected by the spines of the host and are diverse and often large.*
Neville Peat

INVERTEBRATES

Although there have been few invertebrate surveys in the Livingstone, Countess, Dunton and Snowdon uplands, the fauna appears to be highly interesting.

Four species of grasshopper, including the green and orange *Alpinacris tumidicauda* and robust *Sigaus obelisci*, are found in the alpine zone, where they feed on grasses and herbs.

Beetles of note include the giant weevil *Lyperobius spedeni*, which is associated with the small speargrass *Aciphylla lecomtei*, and the large black carabid *Megodromus sandageri*, a voracious predator.

A high-alpine black cicada *Maoricicada nigra frigida* is common in fellfield, where males sing noisily. The species is distributed east to Central Otago.

The majority of moths here are similarly characteristic of Central Otago, with only a few species more closely related to Fiordland. A swift-flying crepuscular species is the handsome grey-and-white hepialid *Aoraia aspina*, a species found east to the Umbrella Mountains.

Geometrid moths are diverse on these ranges, with *Notoreas*

Water birds

Black shags, as keen on fishing the Mavora Lakes as the anglers, are not uncommon here, and with wings outstretched they dry their feathers out while roosting on rocks close to the water.

Marsh crakes, a threatened rail, have been recorded on the lake edges, and Australasian crested grebes have nested by the lake shores.

On the gravel beds of the lower Mararoa River black-fronted dotterels started breeding in about 1980.

New Zealand scaup or papango Aythya novaeseelandiae, *a small duck endemic to New Zealand, is not uncommon on the Mavora Lakes. Scaup are often seen in groups. They are renowned for their diving ability, managing to reach depths of more than 2m with foot propulsion. They feed mainly on small aquatic animals on the lake bed. Nests are made in dense cover by the water's edge.*
Ian Southey

Left and right: *New Zealand's largest alpine casemoth* Orophora unicolor. *The adult males (wingspan 32mm) are strong fliers at dawn, while the females are wingless and remain in the larval/ pupal cocoon where they lay their eggs once mated. The extraordinary larval cases (pictured left), up to 35mm long, are usually adorned with lichens or grass stems. Larvae may take several seasons to reach maturity.*
Brian Patrick

chioneres and *N. galaxias* common by day over herbfield and cushionfield. One species commoner in the western mountains is the small diurnal tortricid *Ascerodes prochlora.* Its polyphagous larvae feed on various herbs including *Dolichoglottis lyallii.*

CARETAKING
Priorities and issues

Chapter 9

On the face of it, Fiordland's size, remoteness and climate would appear to make the region a safe haven for indigenous fauna and flora – a chunk of 'old New Zealand', intact with all its species and abounding in original character. The reality is rather different. Nothing could have prepared the New Zealand biota, not even Fiordland's far-flung communities, for the wholesale assault from predatory and browsing mammals that came with camp followers of human settlers. First to arrive were rats (*Rattus exulans*) and dogs from eastern Polynesia; then came a second and more devastating wave, comprising rats (ship rat *R. rattus* and brown rat *R. norvegicus*), mice, cats, dogs, stoats and deer from Europe, and possums from Australia.

Fiordland's forests, shrublands, grasslands and herbfields took a hammering from red deer. Although deer numbers are much reduced now, as elsewhere in southern New Zealand, a new threat to the flora has arisen since the 1970s in the form of brush-tailed possums invading from north and east. Deer and possums, although selective browsers, can radically alter the make-up of plant communities. Then there are the introduced weeds. So far they have obtained a foothold only at the edges – on the coastal dunes, for example – but footholds have a habit of striding on through an ecosystem. A measure of control is necessary.

Birds and Animals

On the fauna side of things, the picture is gloomier. Trampers often come out of the Fiordland forest deeply puzzled and concerned about why so much of it is bereft of bird song. Flightless or poorly flighted native birds have succumbed to an onslaught from introduced mammals – rats and stoats in particular. Only on those islands lying more than 1.2km from the mainland (or 1.2km from an intermediary stepping-stone island) can native species truly achieve their potential, for virtually all the islands close inshore have been colonised by swimming, tree-climbing rats and stoats. Very few places are safe for endangered species. Breaksea Island and its small consorts nearby are beacons of hope for endangered wildlife in Fiordland, with Centre Island in Lake Te Anau an important refuge in the east. Once an 'island eaten by rats', Breaksea is now a rodent-free refuge for saddlebacks, yellowheads, Fiordland skinks and vulnerable weevils. Refuges can be created. It just takes time, effort and ingenuity.

A new concept introduced in the mid-1990s envisaged the creation of 'mainland islands'. Until then, the focus had been on transferring populations of endangered species, mostly birds,

Wetlands like this one at Redcliff south of Lake Manapouri are models of biodiversity, providing habitat for an array of plants, aquatic invertebrates and birds, some of them rare and special. A Queen Elizabeth II covenant protects the Redcliff wetland, which lies close to the Waiau River. Dewatering of the river by the Manapouri power scheme focused attention on the importance of these associated wetlands. Pedestals of a native sedge, Carex secta, *sprout like busbies from the water.*
Neville Peat

to islands a reasonable distance offshore. The new approach threw open the prospect of sustaining endangered species on the mainland. It involved reducing predator numbers in specified, carefully-selected areas to levels that could be controlled long-term with low-maintenance trapping or poisoning operations. For example, the Eglinton Valley – or part of it – could become a 'mainland island' for long-tailed bat, yellowhead, South Island kaka and South Island robin so long as stoat numbers are kept low and extra efforts are made to contain them following beech-seeding seasons. Although the stoat is the main bête noire of the 1990s, the possum presents a threat to the forest equal to that posed by red deer in the middle of the century. Of lesser concern in Fiordland, but pests all the same, are chamois. The latter are kept in check by helicopter hunting.

Richard Henry

Richard Henry (1845-1929) is the father figure of conservation in Fiordland. Born in Ireland, he settled on the site of present-day Te Anau in 1883 and began exploring the lake and surrounding country.

Recognising his strong interest in birds and nature conservation, the Government appointed him caretaker of Resolution Island – New Zealand's first nature reserve – in 1894, when he was aged 49. From a base at nearby Pigeon Island, Henry pioneered the technique of island transfers of endangered birds. He knew that populations of kakapo were declining rapidly because of predators such as stoats, and in six years, with the aid of a small boat, a muzzled dog and cages, he transferred 350-400 kakapo to islands he considered predator-free. He also transferred large numbers of brown kiwi, little spotted kiwi and weka.

In 1900, to his utter dismay, he saw a stoat on Resolution Island. He resigned that year, believing his work to be ruined by the ability of stoats to swim to islands near the mainland.

His beloved kakapo and little spotted kiwis have disappeared but brown kiwis survive, and the populations on Parrot and Indian Islands in Dusky Sound are probably descended from Henry's transferred birds. There are brown kiwis on Cooper Island, but this population may be natural.

A skilled field naturalist and observer, Henry managed his transfers without the aid of today's technology – radio transmitters, tape-recorders, light-intensifying viewers and helicopters. He stayed on in Dusky Sound till 1909, when he accepted an appointment as custodian of the reserve at Kapiti Island. He is remembered in several Fiordland geographical features – Mt Henry and Henry Saddle (George Sound track), Henry Burn (Seaforth River) and Lake Henry (Te Anau).

Vegetation

Threatened species projects undertaken by the Department of Conservation tend to give priority to fauna, but some plants and vegetation types now figure in protection work, especially around the coast. Plant pests such as gorse, broom, tree lupin and marram grass have yet to spread as widely and densely in Fiordland as they have in many parts of mainland New Zealand, but they are a problem in the making and the Department of Conservation is stepping up efforts to control weeds in the hope of nipping the problem in the bud. The future of the native sand-binder, pingao, on dunelands around the coast depends on how effectively marram grass can be controlled. A grass herbicide is used (pingao is a sedge and not affected). Marram has crept on to dunes and foreshores at some northern bays (Martins and Big Bays, Transit Beach and Catseye Bay) and around the south coast. Eradication is the goal on the south coast sites of Sealers Beach and Big River. The Coal River dunes have been fairly well cleared of marram since it threatened to overwhelm the pingao in the 1980s.

Gorse infestation is also coastal and aided by southward ocean currents. Control operations, based on annual spraying, use helicopters and the DOC vessel *m.v. Renown* to reach the sites. Gorse mites, a form of biological control, have been released into gorse growing on the gravel dunes at Big Bay. European broom and the yellow-flowered tree lupin *Lupinus arboreus*, which reaches 1.5m in height, are causing problems around Lakes Te Anau and Manapouri and at Martins and Big Bays.

Left: *Threatened species research: an intensive study of long-tailed bats in the Eglinton Valley is revealing fascinating new information about the social and breeding behaviour of these small animals, New Zealand's only native terrestrial mammals. Project leader Dr Colin O'Donnell is examining a tagged bat.*
Rod Hay/DoC

Above: *Coal River emerges from behind dark dunes of iron sand 10km north of Breaksea Sound. The dune system here, featuring the orange sand sedge pingao on the foremost dunes, is well preserved thanks to efforts to control infestations of marram grass. In the far south, at Sand Hill Point near Port Craig, is another important dune system.*
Neville Peat

Other introduced weeds posing more localised problems are heather and the conifer species Douglas fir at The Wilderness Scientific Reserve, crack willow at the Mavora Lakes and Himalayan honeysuckle on the Wilmot Pass Road. In the Takitimu Mountains, *Pinus mugo* and *P. contorta* trees that have spread from nearby stabilisation plantings are being considered for removal from the slopes below Tower and Excelsior Peaks where they are threatening native vegetation.

Left: *A boardwalk on the approach to Luxmore Hut on the Kepler Track between Lakes Te Anau and Manapouri. Boardwalking is used to protect wet or seasonally wet vegetation from destruction under trampers' boots.*
Neville Peat

Below: *Understanding underwater life is essential to monitoring the environmental impacts of tourism: a plankton net is secured over a black coral colony in Doubtful Sound in an attempt to understand more about the spawning of the tiny polyps. Eggs were collected in the net as they floated free. From this study, scientists concluded spawning could coincide with a full moon. A butterfly perch swims close, curious.*
Lance Shaw

Tourism

Taking care of Fiordland's fauna, flora and habitats involves more than armed assaults on introduced plants and animals. There is the question of human impacts to consider. Conditions are placed on tourist ventures in Fiordland National Park and adjacent conservation areas. These conditions are designed not only to protect natural values but also to ensure tourism operates on a sustainable basis. After all, Fiordland tourism relies on perpetuating the image of a Shangri-La – a region unsullied by civilisation's worst traits. The challenge for the visitor industry is to move large numbers of people into and out of the region – essentially Milford and Doubtful Sounds – without adversely affecting the Shangri-La atmosphere.

Multi-million-dollar initiatives in the pipeline include the development of a monorail from Wakatipu through Mavora

country and Snowdon Forest to the Milford Road, and, over on the West Coast, the extension of a tourist route south from Haast and the Cascade Valley to the Hollyford, with Milford Sound again the destination. Both projects would need to justify their impacts. The more controversial Cascade-Hollyford road would inevitably involve the use of bulldozers in a national park and the destruction of a strip of primeval lowland forest – an important wilderness. Visitors to Fiordland come by sea, too, mainly on board large cruise ships in summer but also in smaller vessels that allow a more intimate exploration of the fiords. With the modernising and expansion of facilities at Milford Sound, attention is now focusing on development of Doubtful Sound tourism, and for that to happen there will need to be an assessment of the environmental risks as well as the rewards.

Ballast threat

Ships discharging ballast water in or near the fiords can introduce invasive and habitat-wrecking plant species. A red seaweed from Europe, *Polysiphonia brodiaei*, has established in George Sound, presumably as a result of hitch-hiking with a New Zealand-bound vessel. In Dusky Sound and Preservation Inlet is a brown seaweed from Australia, *Sargassum verruculosum*, 1m tall, that was probably introduced by whalers or sealers last century.

The threat of accidental introductions like this has been used as an argument against allowing bulk carriers to export fresh water from Deep Cove, Doubtful Sound, using the discharge from the power scheme tailrace tunnel as the source.

Right: *Vessels making daily cruises on Milford and Doubtful Sounds have been integral to Fiordland tourism, which aims to be sustainable. This vessel is giving visitors a close-up experience of a waterfall in Milford Sound.*
Red Boats

Waitutu Forest

Waitutu, in the far south and outside the national park boundaries, is a case study in conservation. Since the 1970s, there have been urgent calls from the Royal Forest and Bird Protection Society and other quarters to protect formally Waitutu's impressive lowland podocarp/beech forest, a large part of which (2,176ha) is owned by a Maori incorporation. When the owners revealed they had sold cutting rights to the timber, the Government stepped in and began negotiating protection for Waitutu.

In early 1996, a deal was announced. In exchange for protecting Waitutu in perpetuity and allowing it to be managed by DoC as if it were part of Fiordland National Park, the Waitutu Incorporation (800 members) was to be paid $13.55 million over several years and, in addition, gain compensatory cutting rights to 11,582ha of Crown beech forest in the Longwood Range, Rowallan and Woodlaw forests. Although this alternative logging must be conducted on a sustainable management basis, the prospect irks conservationists. The biggest area earmarked for logging is in Rowallan forest on slopes facing the sawmilling town of Tuatapere. When the national park boundaries were set, Rowallan and Dean forests between Waitutu and the Waiau River were excluded on account of the 'merchantable timber' they contained. Subsequently, large areas of these forests were clearfelled for sawlogs and woodchips. South Island kaka and yellowhead populations virtually disappeared from the cut-over areas. Some parts of Rowallan and Dean forests enjoy formal protection, however. In the middle of Rowallan forest is a magnificent podocarp stand, the Lindsay Scientific Reserve, in which large totara are a feature. Dean forest, to the north, has a few giant totara trees approaching 1,000 years in age.

Grazing

While logging has been a major issue in the south, grazing has been no less controversial in the north. There are two contentious areas – the Eglinton Valley (sheep) and the Mavora Lakes (cattle). Sheep have grazed the river flats in the Eglinton Valley since 1859. Following the gazettal of Fiordland National Park in 1952, the owners of Te Anau Downs Station were licensed to continue grazing, but in 1975 a 21-year licence was issued to give the graziers time to develop their own property and ultimately withdraw their sheep from the Eglinton flats. The 1991 park management plan confirmed the phasing out of sheep – a policy that continues to be embroiled in argument. To the east, cattle traditionally seasonally graze the tussock grasslands adjacent to North Mavora Lake. This licensed use of conservation land has raised the hackles of groups and individuals who object to the degrading of native vegetation through grazing and trampling.

Right: Landscapes are important in conservation terms. Adjacent to West Cape, the remotest part of mainland New Zealand, is a tract of uplifted land, hillocky in places but flat overall compared to the steep glaciated terrain further east. This peneplain extends inland for about 8km between Dusky Sound and Chalky Inlet. It is crisscriossed by narrow incised valleys. An old marine bench 30m above sea level has been identified here. Forest grows in the valleys but the flatter surfaces are generally covered by tussock grassland dominated by the needle-leaved snow grass Chionochloa acicularis.
Alan Mark

The grazing issues, not to mention logging and marine reserves, represent a clash of ethics. A rising conservation ethic is confronting an ethic based on traditional rights, economic development and a fairly liberal access to natural resources. Fiordland is not the only place where these ethics clash, of course. But because of the scale, grandness and preciousness of Fiordland, it always seems that the issues loom large.

Possum plague

Possums represent the greatest threat to New Zealand's forests and forest fauna. There are now more possums than sheep – some 70 million. They consume an estimated 20,000 tonnes of fruit, seed, leaves and stems per day, causing dieback in some forests and competing with birds for food. They also prey on birds' eggs.

Although possums were released (for a fur industry) at Dusky, Doubtful and Dagg Sounds in the 1890s and they have invaded much of Fiordland, there are a few areas that are thought to be possum-free – probably the only areas of lowland forest in New Zealand never touched by possums. This unique record has given impetus to possum control operations based on a mixture of trapping and poisoning (bait stations) at strategic places.

One of the sites for possum control is the bulging peninsula centred on Mt Forbes (1,305m), between Doubtful and Dagg Sounds. It is connected to the mainland by a neck of land less than 2km wide (between Crooked Arm and Dagg Sound). Although possums were liberated at Dagg Sound, they appear to have died out, possibly because of the climate. Further south, large areas around Preservation and Chalky Inlets are free of possums or virtually free of them. Possums have colonised the Waitutu area and moved westwards as far as Big River. Apparently they gained access to Waitutu by sneaking across the Waitutu River swing bridge. They may also have negotiated their way over log jams during low flows in the Waitutu River. Possums can swim but they are reluctant to enter water.

Marine reserves

Ironically, the national park boundaries do not include the water of the fiords, despite the sea's association with the fiord landscape. At present, Fiordland National Park stops at the high tide mark. Two small marine reserves break the pattern, though. The larger, covering 690ha of Milford Sound, protects rock-wall communities on the north side of the sound. The reserve is called Piopiotahi, the Maori name for Milford Sound. The other marine reserve, occupying 93ha, spans Te Awaatu Channel in Doubtful Sound, between Secretary and Bauza Islands. Although small, the reserves represent a move towards more extensive protection for the special life forms and habitats of the fiords. The sea is the conservation movement's new frontier. In a region such as Fiordland, the site of New Zealand's largest national park and one of its oldest, the case for a network of marine reserves bordering the protected land is especially compelling. A continuum is thus created. On a geological timescale, the tide mark is but a temporary boundary anyway. Sea levels rise and fall, and the land itself moves. Besides the fiords, potential sites for marine reserves in Fiordland are the Solander Islands and the Waitutu coast.

Te Awaatu Channel, Doubtful Sound, where a marine reserve protects life in the fiord.
Neville Peat

BIBLIOGRAPHY

Adams N M, 1994. *Seaweeds of New Zealand.* Canterbury University Press.

Barlow B A, 1986. *Flora and Fauna of Alpine Australasia.* Ages and Origins. CSIRO.

Bishop G and Forsyth J, 1988. *Vanishing Ice.* John McIndoe/New Zealand Geological Survey.

Burrows C J and Dobson A T, 1972. *Mires of the Manapouri-Te Anau Lowlands.* New Zealand Ecological Society. Proceedings Vol. 19:75-99.

Butler D, 1989. *Quest for the Kakapo.* Heinemann Reed.

Clarke C E, 1934. *The Lepidoptera of the Te Anau-Manapouri Lakes Districts.* Transactions of the New Zealand Institute. Vol. 63:112-132.

Cooper W J, MisKelly C M, Morrison K and Peacock R J, 1986. *Birds of the Solander Islands,* Notornis 33, 77-89.

Department of Lands and Survey, 1986. *Mountains of Water – The Story of Fiordland National Park.*

Elliot G, 1986. Mohua – A Declining Species. *Forest & Bird.* Vol. 17:26-28.

Elliot G P and Ogle C, 1985. *Wildlife and Wildlife Habitat Values of Waitutu Forest Western Southland.* Fauna Survey Unit Report 39, NZ Wildlife Service.

Forsyth J, Turnbull I, Lee B and Beecroft G, 1991. *A Guide to the Kepler Track.* John McIndoe/DSIR.

Gaskin C and Peat N, 1991. *The World of Penguins.* Hodder & Stoughton.

Gaskin C and Peat N, 1991. *The World of Albatrosses.* Hodder & Stoughton.

Grange K, 1986. The Underwater World of Fiordland. *Forest & Bird.* Vol. 17:10-13.

Grange K, Singleton R J, Goldberg W M, Hill P J, 1991. *The Underwater Environment of Doubtful Sound.* New Zealand Oceanographic Institute.

Grange K and Goldberg W, 1993. Fiords Down Under. *Natural History,* March.

Hall-Jones G (Editor), 1960. *Handbook to the Fiordland National Park* 1st Edition. Fiordland National Park Board.

Hall-Jones J, 1979. *Fiordland Place Names.* Fiordland National Park Board.

Hall-Jones J, 1989. Kakapo Tracks at George Sound. *Forest & Bird.* Vol. 20:20-21.

Hare J, Hayes S and King S. *1990 Southland Conservancy Coastal Resource Inventory* (First Order Survey). Department of Conservation, Wellington.

Heads M J, 1994. A Biogeographic review of Parahebe (*Scrophulariaceae*). *Biological Journal of the Linnean Society.* Vol. 115:65-89.

Heads M J, 1994. Biogeography and Evolution in the *Hebe* Complex (*Scrophulariaceae*): *Leonohebe* and *Chionohebe. Candollea.* Vol. 49:21-119.

Heads M J, 1994. Biogeography and Biodiversity in New Zealand *Pimelea* (*Thymelaeaceae*). *Candollea.* Vol. 49:37-53.

Higham T, 1992. Pekapeka. New Zealand's Secretive Bats. 1992 *Forest & Bird.* No. 265:21-26.

Hill S and J, 1987. *Richard Henry of Resolution Island.* John McIndoe.

Homer, Lloyd and Molloy, Les 1988. *The Fold of the Land.* Allen & Unwin, Wellington.

Howes W G, 1946. Lepidoptera Collecting at the Homer, with descriptions of New Species. *Transactions of the Royal Society of New Zealand.* Vol. 76:139-147.

Hutching G, 1985. World Heritage – South-West New Zealand. *Forest & Bird,* Vol. 16:2-4.

Hutching G and Potton C (eds), 1987. *Forest, Fiords & Glaciers.* Royal Forest and Bird Protection Society.

Hutchins L, 1984. Mavora Lakes – National Reserve or Pastoral Park. *Forest & Bird.* Vol. 15:6.

Johnson P N, 1972. *Vegetation of Lake Manapouri Shoreline.* New Zealand Ecological Society. Proceedings Vol. 19:102-119.

Johnson P N, 1975. Vegetation and flora of Solander Islands, Southern New Zealand. *New Zealand Journal of Botany.* Vol. 13:189-214.

Johnson P N, 1979. *Vegetation of Fiordland Beaches.* DSIR, Dunedin.

Johnson P N, 1982. Botanical Notes on Some Southern New Zealand Islands. *New Zealand Journal of Botany.* Vol. 20:121-130.

Johnson P N, 1992. *The Sand Dune and Beach Vegetation Inventory of New Zealand. II South Island and Stewart Island.* DSIR. Land Resources Scientific Report No. 16.

Jolly V H and Brown J M A (eds), 1975. *New Zealand Lakes.* Auckland University Press/Oxford University Press.

Lee B and Lavers R, 1990. *Chionochloa spiralis,* Fiordland's Forgotten Tussock. *Forest & Bird.* Vol. 22:34-41

Lee D E, 1983. An Oligocene rocky shore community from Mt Luxmore, Fiordland. *NZ Journal of Geology and Geophysics.* Vol. 26.

Lee W G and Given D R, 1984. *Celmisia spedenii* G Simpson an Ultramafic Endemic and *Celmisia markii* sp. from Southern New Zealand. *New Zealand Journal of Botany.* Vol. 22:585-592.

Livingstone M E, Biggs B J, and Gifford J S, 1986. *Inventory of NZ Lakes Part II, South Island.* National Water and Soil Conservation Authority.

McDowall R M, 1981. *Freshwater Fish in Fiordland National Park.* Fisheries Environmental Report No.12, Ministry of Agriculture and Fisheries.

McGlone M S and Bathgate J L, 1983. Vegetation and Climate History of the Longwood Range, South Island, New Zealand, 12,000 BP to the Present. *New Zealand Journal of Botany.* Vol. 21:293-316.

McLellan E D, 1990. Distribution of Stoneflies in New Zealand. In I C Campbell (ed.) *Mayflies and Stoneflies.* 135-140.

Mark A F, 1975. Lakes Manapouri and Te Anau. *New Zealand Nature Heritage.* pp 2877-2884.

Mark A F, 1989. Responses of Indigenous Vegetation to Contrasting Trends in Utilisation by Red Deer in two South-western New Zealand National Parks. *New Zealand Journal of Ecology.* Vol. 12:103-114.

Mark A F and Adams N M, 1995. *New Zealand Alpine Plants.* 4th Edition. Godwit.

Mark A F and Baylis G T S, 1975. Impact of Deer on Secretary Island, Fiordland, New Zealand. *Proceedings of the New Zealand Ecological Society.* Vol. 22:19-24.

Mark A F, Rawson G and Wilson J B, 1979. Vegetation Pattern of a Lowland Raised Mire in Eastern Fiordland, New Zealand. *New Zealand Journal of Ecology.* Vol. 2:1-10.

Mills J A, Lavers R B and Lee W G, 1984. The Takahe – A Relic of the Pleistocene Grassland Avifauna of New Zealand. *New Zealand Journal of Ecology.* Vol. 7:57-70.

Morrison J V, 1982. Fiordland National Park – a new locality for the divaricating shrub *Pittosporum obcordatum* Raoul. *New Zealand Journal of Botany*. Vol. 20:195-196.

Murphy E C and Dowding J E, 1995. Ecology of the Stoat in *Nothofagus* forest: Home range, habitat use and diet at different stages of the beech mast cycle. *New Zealand Journal of Ecology*. Vol. 19 No. 2.

Mutch A R, 1972. Geology of the Morley Subdivision. *New Zealand Geographical Survey Bulletin 78*.

New Zealand Geological Survey, 1989. *A Guide to Milford Sound*. DSIR Pamphlet.

O'Connor K F, Batchelor G W and Davison J, 1982. *Mavora*. Centre for Resource Management, Lincoln College.

Patrick B H, 1995. Reaffirmation of the type locality of Stokells Smelt in Southland. *Journal of the Royal Society of New Zealand*. Vol. 25(1):95-97.

Patrick B H, Rance B D, Barratt B I P and Tangney R, 1987. *Entomological Survey of Longwood Range*. Department of Conservation.

Patrick B H, Rance B D, Lyford B and Barratt B I P, 1987. *Entomological Survey of Snowdon Peak*. Department of Conservation.

Pillai A, 1991. Fiordland, Protecting the Undersea World. *Forest & Bird*. Vol. 22:34-41.

Riddell D C, Freestone H and Nutting S, 1993. *Waiau River Hydrology*. Southland Regional Council.

Tangney R S, Wilson J B and Mark A F, 1990. Bryophyte Island Biogeography: A Study in Lake Manapouri, New Zealand. *Oikos*. Vol. 59:21-26.

Thomas B and Taylor R, 1988. Rat Eradication in Breaksea Sound. *Forest & Bird*. Vol. 19:30-34.

Turnbull I M, Uruski C I et al, 1993. *Cretaceous and Cenozoic Sedimentary Basins of Western Southland, South Island, New Zealand*. Institute of Geological and Nuclear Sciences. Monograph 1.

Turnbull I M, 1996. *Geology of the Waitutu, Rowallan and Dean Forests, Western Southland*. Institute of Geological and Nuclear Sciences.

Ward C M, Mark A F, Grealish G, Wilson J B, Tangney R S, Ogle C, Patrick B H and Mason G M, 1988. The Geology, Flora and Fauna of the Waitutu Marine Terraces. Collected Papers from the *Journal of the Royal Society of New Zealand*. No. 4.

Wardle P, Mark A F and Baylis G T S, 1973. Vegetation and Landscape of the West Cape District, Fiordland, New Zealand. *New Zealand Journal of Botany* Vol.11.

Wellman H W and Willett R W, 1942. The Geology of the West Coast from Abut Head to Milford Sound – Part 1. *Transactions and Proceedings of the Royal Society of New Zealand*. Vol. 71:282-306.

White J and Hall-Johns J, 1981. *New Zealand's Majestic Wilderness*. Orakau House.

Wilson H and Galloway T, 1993. *Small-leaved Shrubs of New Zealand*. Manuka Press.

Wilson H, 1982. *Stewart Island Plants*. Field Guide Publications.

Winterbourn M J and Gregson U L D, 1989. Guide to the Aquatic Insects of New Zealand. *Bulletin of the Entomological Society of New Zealand. No. 9.*

INDEX

Fgures in italics refer to illustrations

Aan River 19
Abrotanella rostrata 57
Acanthisitta chloris see rifleman, South
  Island
Acianthus fornicatus 47
Aciphylla 10, 52, 57-8, 72, 114
  aff *glaucescens* 40, *48*
  congesta 58, 61, 70, *100*
  crenulata 58
  crosby-smithii 58, *101*
  divisa 58, 61
  horrida 58, 113, 121, *122*
  lecomtei 121, *122*
  leighii 58
  lyallii 58, 60, 112
  multisecta 58
  pinnatifida 58, 121
  scott-thomsonii 58
  spedenii 58
  takahea 12, 58
Acrocladium cuspidatum 47
Actinotus novaezelandiae 115
Agrostis capillaris 40
Ailsa Mountains 72
Alepis flavida 96
Aletia argentaria 49
  nobilia 69
algae 21
Alpinacris tumidicauda 13, *103*, 122
Alpine Fault 19, 22-3, 50
Amphikonophora giganteus 70, *73*
Anagotus 85
  fairburni 4, 85
  oconnori 104
Anas aucklandica chlorotis see teal,
  brown
Anatidae 44
Anchor Island *75*, 82
Androstoma empetrifolia 40, 47
Anguilla dieffenbachii 38
Anisotome 72
  capillifolia 121
  flexuosa 60, *70*
  haastii 60, 61, 72
  lyallii 56, 72, *85*, 87, *88*, 89
  pilifera 61, 121
Anthornis melanura see bellbird
Antipathes fiordensis see coral, black
Aoraia aspina 113, 122
  aurimaculata 70
  dinodes 48, 70, 116
Aponotoreas incompta 114
  insignis 114
  orphnaea 114
  synclinalis 103, *116*
  villosa 103, 117
Apteryoperla illiesi 68, 105

  monticola 105
  ramsayi 105
  tillyardi 105
Apteryx australis see kiwi, South Island
  brown
Arachnocampa luminosa 39
Arctocephalus forsteri see seal, NZ fur
Ardea novaehollandiae 45
Aristotelia fruticosa 113
arrow grass 88
Asaphodes cinnabari 48
  sericodes 113
Ascarina lucida 87
Ascerodes prochlora 123
Asplenium obtusatum 89
Astelia 61
  linearis 115
  nervosa 47, 54
  nivicola 54, *104*
  subulata 115
Asterivora barbigera 114
Astrobrachion constrictum 79
Athoracophorus 73
Atomotricha prospiciens 117
Aurora Caves 20
Australian Plate 22
Austrofestuca littoralis 56
Austrolestes colensonis 44
Austroperla cyrene 68
Austrosimulium 71
  australense 71
  ungulatum 71
Awarua River 56
Aythya novaeseelandiae see scaup, NZ

Back Valley 100, 107
Bald Hill *114*, 115
bat, long-tailed 12, 40, 43, *43*, 126-7
  short-tailed 43, 81
Baumea 47
  rubiginosa 44
  tenax 44
Bauza Island 132
beech, mountain 34, 36, 54, *93*, 96-7
  red *11*, 40, 96
  silver 36, 54, *94*, 96-7
beetle, carabid *68*, 116
  chafer 103
  stag *104*
  see also weevil
bellbird 12, 52, 91, 107, 117, 196
Belle, Mt 30
Big Bay *9*, 55, 56, 127
Big River *65*, 95, 127, 131
biogeography 13
bittern, Australasian 44, 55
Black Lake 59, 60, 61, *61*

blackfly (sandfly) 11, 71, *71*
Blackmount Hills 19
Blechnum discolor 97, *115*
Bligh Sound *50*
Borland Mire 45
Borland Saddle *9*, *94*, *96*, *100*, *101*
Borland Valley *9*, 45
Botaurus poiciloptilus see bittern,
  Australasian
Bowdleria punctata see fernbird, South
  Island
Bowen Channel 83
Bowen Falls 76
brachiopods 21, *78*, 79
Brachyglottis bellidioides 121
  revolutus 60, 121
  rotundifolia 56, 89
  stewartiae 89
Brachyscome linearis 33
Bradshaw Sound 74
Breaksea Island *10*, 82, 84-6, 88, 107,
  124
Breaksea Sound 22, 72, *82, 84*, 84-5,
  88, 92, *104*, *127*
broadleaf 36, 87, 97
Brod Bay 34
brown creeper 42, 106-7, 117
Browne Falls 76
browntop 40
bryozoa 21
Bubulcus ibis see egret, cattle
bug 13, 68
Bulbinella gibbsii balanifera 60
  modesta 87
bully, red-finned 38
  upland 113
Burns, Mt *100*, *101*
Burwood Bush 42, 48, 67
buttercup 56
butterfly, black *9*, 113
  copper 60

caddis 68, *70*, 104
Cadman, Lake *27*
Callaeas cinerea see kokako, South
  Island
Calloria inconspicua 79
Calystegia soldanella 56
Cameron Mountains 95, 102
Campylopus kirkii 47
Cardamine 122
Carex 44, 47
  diandra 44
  gaudichaudiana 34, 44
  pleiostachys 87
  pumila 56
  secta 125

sinclairii 44
Carmichaelia arborea 54, *61*
 juncea 35
 lacustris 35
Caroline Peak 27
Carpha alpina 47, 116
Carrick, Lake *27*
Cascade River 87
Cascade Saddle 102
Cascade Valley 129
casemoth, alpine 123
Cassinia 103, 121
 vauvilliersii 47, 49, 113, 115
Caswell Sound 19, 76
Catharacta skua lonnbergi see skua,
 brown
Catseye Bay *50*, 127
celery pine *40*, 121
Celmisia 10
 aff *gracilenta* 47
 coriacea 115
 densiflora 112, 121
 durietzii 60
 glandulosa 45, 115, 121
 hectorii *60*, 121
 holosericea 11, 87
 inaccessa *101*
 markii 121
 petriei 13, 66, 113
 praestans *101*
 semicordata 60
 semicordata var *stricta* *111*, 112, 121
 spedenii *121*
 traversii 13, *101*
 verbascifolia 60
 viscosa 13
 walkeri 60, *64*, 121
Centre Island 32, 124
Centre Pass *64*
Centrolepis ciliata 46, 115
 minima 115
Cephalorhynchus hectori see dolphin,
 Hector's
Cerberus, Mt *121*
Cermatulus nasalis 113
chafer 113
chaffinch 52
Chalinolobus tuberculatus see bat, long-
 tailed
Chalky Inlet 16, *27*, 72, 74, *78*, 85, 92,
 130, 131
Chalky Island *17*, 85
Cheimarrichthys fosteri 39, 113
chickweed, cushion 56
 scree 112
Chionochloa 10, 57, 102-3
 acicularis 102-3, 130
 conspicua 103
 crassiuscula 66
 crassiuscula directa 103, 115

crassiuscula torta 103, 115
 macra 103, 112, 121
 oreophila 61, *100*, 103
 ovata 102-3
 pallens 102
 pallens cadens 59, 66, 103, 112, 115
 rigida 103, 112, 121
 rigida amara 59, 66, 102-3
 rubra cuprea 44, 48, *48*, 103, 115
 spiralis 102, 102-3
 teretifolia *102*, 102-3, 115
 vireta 103
Chionogentias lineata 116
 montana 61
Christaperla eylesi 105
Christina, Mt 50
cicada, black *69*, 114, 122
Circus approximans see harrier, Australasian
Cladonia 96
Clare Peak *111*
Cleddau River 70
Cleddau Valley 52
Cleughearn Peak 103
Clinton River 30
Coal River 86, *100*, *127*
cod, blue *78*
 red 78
Colobanthus buchananii 112
Commander Peak 74
Cook, Captain James 11, 71, 80, 91
Cookia 21
 sulcata 21
Cooper Island 106, 126
Coprosma 36, 55, 57, 60-61
 acerosa 56
 cuneata 47
 foetidissima 97
 parviflora 49
 petriei 49
 propinqua 88
 pseudocuneata 60
 serrulata 60
coprosma, sand 56
coral, black *9*, *78*, *79*, 128
 red *9*
Coriaria sarmentosa 49
Corinuncia variegata granulata 117
Corokia cotoneaster 47, 49
Cortaderia richardii 40
Costachorema hebdomon *104*
Countess Peak 120
Countess Range 118, 120
crake, marsh 113, 123
Crassula helmsii 88
 moschata 88
crayfish, freshwater 117
cricket, black 49
Crooked Arm 131
Cunaris Sound *78*

cushion plants *120*
Cyanoramphus auriceps see parakeet,
 yellow-crowned
 malherbi see parakeet, orange-
 fronted
 novaeseelandiae see parakeet, red-
 crowned
Cyathodes 61
 juniperina 97, 104
Cyperus ustulatus 87

Dacrycarpus dacrydioides see kahikatea
Dacrydium cupressinum see rimu
Dagg Sound 131
Darran Mountains *25*, 50, 52, *55*, *58*,
 73, 105
Dasyuris 68, 70
 anceps 70
 callicrena 68
 fulminea *12*, 68
 leucobathra 114
 octans 70
 transaurea 48
Dean Forest 19, 130
Declana glacialis 114
Deep Cove 9, 14, 28, 30, 32, 74, 129
Deinacrida connectens 112, 113
Delphinus delphis see dolphin, common
Deschampsia caespitosa 34
Desmoschoenus spiralis 55, 56, 89
Dicksonia squarrosa 97
diorite 18
Dioxycanus fuscus 116
Diporochaeta aquatica 32
Discaria toumatou 47, *48*
Dismal Swamp 47
Divide, The *25*, 30, 50
dobsonfly 43
Dolichoglottis lyallii 57, 116, 123
 scorzoneroides 57, *57*, 69
dolphin, bottlenose *9*, 80, *81*
 common 80
 dusky 80
 Hector's 80, 109, *109*
Dome Mire 47
Donatia novae-zelandiae 115
Donne Glacier *27*
dotterel, black-fronted 123
 NZ 11
Doubtful Sound 9, 14, 21, 30, 65, 74,
 80, *81*, 82, 105, *108*, *128*, 129, 131-2,
 132
Dracophyllum 121
 fiordense 9, 54, *55*
 longifolium 84, 87, 113, 115
 menziesii 60, *61*, 99
 muscoides 13
 oliveri *40*, 44
 pearsonii 115
 prostratum *40*, 121

uniflorum 49, *111*, 113, 121
dragonfly 44, *45*
Drosera arcturi 40
    spathulata 40
duck, blue 11, 108, *108*
    grey 36, 44, 108
Dunton Range 118
Dusky Fault 19, 23
Dusky Sound 11, 14, 19, 23, 39, 64, 72,
    74-5, 83, 84, 85, 92, 94, 106-7, 129,
    130, 130-31
Dusky Track 108
Dysphyma australe 89

Earina autumnalis 36, *37*
    mucronata 36
earthquakes 19
earthworm 12, 32, 117
Easter orchid *37*
echinoids 21
ecological districts 14
    regions 14
edelweiss 112
    South Island 57-8, *58*
Edpercivalia harrisoni 104
    spaini 68
Edwardson Sound 27, 72
eel, long-finned 38
Eglinton River 30, *38*
Eglinton Valley 18, 25, 39-40, 50, 42-3,
    43, 86, 126-7, 130
egret, cattle 44-5
Eldon, Mt 22
Empodisma minus 40, 44, 103, 115
Epilobium crassum 122
    matthewsii 100
    porphyrium 60, 121
    tasmanicum 112
Esk Burn 30
Eucamptodon inflatus 47
Eudyptula minor see penguin, blue
Eudyptes pachyrhynchus see Fiordland,
    crested
Euphorbia glauca 10, 56, *89*
Euphrasia repens 87
Excelsior Peak 127
Exsul singularis see fly, bat-winged

falcon, NZ 11, 40, 52, 106
fantail, South Island 91, 106, 117
feather star *78*
Fergus, Lake 30, 39
fern, crown 97, 115
    tangle 47
fernbird, South Island 45, 56, 113
Five Fingers Peninsula 82, *75*, 79, 84,
    87, *88*
flax 88
    mountain 115
fly, bat-winged 70, *72*

Forbes, Mt 131
forget-me-not 56
Forster, George 11, 82
Forster, Johann 11
Forster, Lake 87
Forstera sedifolia 57
fossils 16
Freycinetia baueriana banksii see kiekie
Front Islands 83

gabbro 18
Gaimardia setacea 115
Gair Loch 108
Galaxias argenteus 11, 38, *38*, 56, 113
    brevipinnis 38
    fasciatus 38
    maculatus 38
    paucispondylus 113
    postvectis 97
    vulgaris 38
galaxiid, common river 38
Gallirallus australis see weka, western
    australis scotti see weka, Stewart
    Island
gannet, Australasian 12, 90
Gaultheria 57, 61
    depressa 47, 49
    macrostigma 47
    rupestris 36
Gelophaula triscula 68
Geodorcus helmsi *104*, 116
    philpotti 104
George, Lake 113
George Sound *50*, 129
Geotria australis 39
Geranium sessiliflorum var a*renarium* 56
Gertrude Saddle *57*, *59*, 61, 72
Gertrude Valley 59, *59*, *61*
Gingidia decipiens 112
Glacier Creek 27
Gleichenia dicarpa 47, 115
glow-worm 39, *39*
Glyphipterix aenea 117
Gobiomorphus breviceps 113
    huttoni 38
Gondwana 18, 22
Goose Cove 79
goose, Canada 44
Gorge, The 48, *48*
Grammitis rigida 87
granite 18
Graphania maya 69
    nullifera 122
    oliveri 69
graptolites 16, *16*
grass, marram 126
grasshopper *see Sigaus, Alpinacris*
Gratiola nana 34
grayling 39
Grebe River 30, *30*

Grebe Valley *30*, 106
grebe, Australasian crested 36, 123
Green Lake 30, 73
Griselinia littoralis 36, 97
    lucida 87
gull, red-billed 90
    southern black-backed 90
Gunn, Lake 30, 39

Haastia sinclairii 60, *61*, 112, 121
Hadramphus stilbocarpae see weevil,
    knobbled
Haematopus unicolor see oyster-catcher,
    variable
Hakapoua, Lake 23, 95
hakoakoa *see skua, brown*
Haliotis 20, 21
Hall Arm 74
Halocarpus bidwillii 44, *47*, 49, *49*, 115-
    116
    biformis 97, 114
Halticoperla tara 68
Hamley Peak 105
harebell 56
Harmologa festiva 103
    pontifica 13
    sanguinea 103
harrier, Australasian 45
harvestmen 12, 117
haumakaroa 97
Hauroko Fault 19, 23
Hauroko, Lake 9, 19-20, *23*, 27, 30, 83,
    95, *95*, 97, *99*, 106
Hawea Island *4*, 82, 84-5, *84*, 104
Hebe 102-3, 113
    buchananii 121
    canterburiensis 99
    cockayneana 12, 60, 68
    crawii 110
    elliptica 84, 87, 89
    haastii var *humilis* 113
    rakaiensis 113
    subalpina 60, 121
Hectorella caespitosa 121
Hedycarya arborea 87
Helichrysum bellidioides 60
Heloxycanus patricki 44, 116
Hemideina crassidens 68, 70
Henry Burn 126
Henry Saddle 126
Henry, Lake 126
Henry, Mt 126
Henry, Richard 36, 39, 107, 126
heron, white 36, 44
    white-faced 36, 44-5
Herpolirion novae-zelandiae 49
Hilda, Lake 30
Hoheria lyallii 59, *59*
Holcoperla angularis 68, *68*, 70, *105*
holly, mountain 115

Hollyford Fault 19, 23
Hollyford River 27, 55, *55*, 70, 80
Hollyford Valley 9, 18, 25, 30, 50, 52-3, *53, 57,* 59, 106, 129
Home Creek *46*
Homer Cirque 9, 59, 64
Homer Tunnel 30, 50, 52-3, 59, 64, 68-9, 72
Hope Arm 100
Hoplodactylus granulatus 86
    maculatus 86
horoeka 36
Hump, The *23, 99,* 103, 104
Hunter Mountains 13, *29,* 73, 86, 103-4
hutu 87
Hydatella inconspicua 34
Hydrocotyle novaezealandiae 56
Hymenolaimus malacorhynchos see duck, blue
Hypericum sp *47*
Hypolepis millefolium 66

ice ages 19
iceplant 89
igneous *18*
inaka 84, 87, 114
inanga 38
Island Lake 30, *94*
Isoetes alpinus 33
Isolepis cernua 88
    nodosa 56
Isthmus Sound 83
Iti lacustris 33
Izatha mira 117

Jackson Bay 73
John O'Groats River 50
Johnson, Peter 33

kahikatea *35,* 36, *99*
Kaikoura Orogeny 19
Kaipo River 87
kaka, South Island 40, 56, 84, 106, 126, 130
kakapo 92, *107,* 126
kakariki 91, 106, 117
kamahi 87, 97
karoro 90
karst 21
karuhiruhi *see* shag, pied
kea 52, 64-5, *65*
Kelleria croizatii 61, *69,* 103, 112, 121
    dieffenbachii 115
    palulosa 121
    villosa 13, 121
Kepler Mire *46,* 47
Kepler Mountains 50, 102-3
Kepler Track *11, 20,* 21, 96, *128*
Key Summit 25

kiekie 84, *87*
Kikihia new species 116
    rosea 68
Kirkianella novae-zelandiae 121
Kiwi Burn 95
Kiwi, Lake 95
kiwi, little spotted 126
    South Island brown 66, 84, 126
knobby clubrush 56
koaro 38, 97
kohuhu 36
kokako, South Island 11, 92, 106
kokopu, banded 38, *97*
    giant 11, 38, *38,* 56, 113
    short-jawed *97*
korora 90
korure 83, 90
kowhai *29,* 35
kuaka 90

Lady of the Snows *50*
Lagarostrobus colensoi 47
Lagenifera pumila 56
Lagenorhynchus obscurus see dolphin, dusky
lamprey 39
lancewood 36, 97
Larus dominicanus see gull, southern black-backed
    novaehollandiae scopulinus see gull, red-billed
leatherwood 97, 115
Leonohebe 100, 103
    aff *odora* 115
    annulata 113
    hectorii 60, 100, 121
    laingii 100
    mooreae 60, *112,* 115
    odora 49, 115
    pauciflora 100
    pauciramosa 116, 121
    petriei 100
    petriei murrellii 100
Lepidium oleraceum 89
Lepidoperca tasmanica 78
Lepidoptera 68
Lepidothamnus intermedius 47, 96-7
    laxifolius 47, 116
Leptinella goyenii 13
Leptocarpus similis 34, 88
Leptospermum scoparium see manuka
Leucogenes grandiceps 57, *58,* 112
Leucopogon 61
    colensoi 49
    fraseri 49
Lilaeopsis novaezealandie 88
limestone 19, 20, *20, 21,* 101, 102
Lindsay Scientific Reserve 130.
Liothyrella neozelandica 79
Little Red Hills 22

Little Solander 89-90
Livingstone Fault 19, 23, 120
Livingstone Mountains 9, 13, *22, 69,* 72, 100, 102, 112, 118-21, *119, 120*
Long Reef 55
Long Sound 101
long-finned eel 38
Longwood Range 9, 13, 18, 30, 38, 57, 102-3, 110, 113-17, *114, 115,* 130
Loxomeris 68
Luxmore Hut *128*
Luxmore, Mt 20-21, *20,* 68, 86, *101,* 102
Lycaena boldenarum 60
    salustius 60
Lyperobius 72, 114
    coxalis 72, 103
    cupiendus 72
    hudsoni 72
    undescribed new species 70, 72
    spedeni 72, 122
Lyvia River 108

McKenzie Lagoon 55
McKenzie, Lake *52*
McKerrow, Lake 30, 55, *55,* 68, 76, 80
Mackinnon Pass *2-3*
Madeline, Mt 50
Mahara Island *37*
mahoe 84, 87
makomako 52, 107
mallard 36, 44
Manapouri Power Scheme 9, 45
Manapouri, Lake 9, 25, *25,* 28, *29,* 30, 32, *32-3,* 35, 36, *37,* 44, 47, 53, 65, 86, 97, 100, 106-7, 120, *125,* 127, *128*
manuka 11, *32,* 34, 44, 49, *93,* 97
Maoricicada nigra 69
    nigra frigida 122
    oromelaena 69
    otagoenesis macewini 114
mapou 36, 97
Mararoa catchment 32
Mararoa River 28, 30, 49, 118, *119,* 123
Marsippospermum gracile 121
marine reserves 132
marine fossils 19
marine terraces 23
marram *50*
marsh crake 45
marsh marigold 57
Martins Bay 9, 55, *55,* 76, 127
Mary Island 95
matagouri *47, 48*
matai 36
matuku 44
Mavora Lakes 9, 22, 30, 32, 113, 118-20, *119,* 123, 127, 130
Mavora Lakes Conservation Park 120
Mecodema rex 116

Megadromus sandageri 122
Megaleptoperla grandis 68
Metacrias erichrysa 69
   strategica 48
Meterana meyricci 48
Metrosideros fulgens 87
   perforata 87
   umbellata 36, 87
Microlaena thomsonii 115
Milford Glacier 27
Milford Road 9, 30, 50, 52, *53*, 59, 129
Milford Sound 9, 14, *14*, 22, 27, *27*, 40,
   50, *50*, 52, *57*, 74, 81, 87, 107, 128-9,
   132
Milford Track *2-3*, *13*, 50, 64, 72
milkweed 56, *89*
mingimingi 97, 104
miro 36, 97
mistletoe *96*, 117
Mitre Peak *9*, 50
Mohoua albicilla *see* whitehead
   novaeseelandiae *see* brown creeper
   ochrocephala *see* yellowhead
mohua *see* yellowhead
mollymawk, southern Buller's 83, *90*
   white-capped or shy *83*
Monk, Lake 95
Monkey Creek 53, *57*
Monowai catchment 32
Monowai, Lake 19, 30, 32, 36, 86, 103,
   106
Moonlight Fault 19, 23
Morus serrator *see* gannet, Australasian
Moth, Aoraia 43
   giant 70
   tiger 69
   diurnal 12 *see also Notoreas, Dasyuris,*
   Paranotoreas, Aponotoreas
   see Proteodes, Graphania
Mount Aspiring National Park 22
Muehlenbeckia axillaris 59, *60*
Murchison Mountains 12-13, *12*, *20*,
   52, *55*, 58, 66-7, 69, 72, 100, 102-4,
   102, 106
Mustela erminea 42
muttonbird 12
muttonbird shrub 56, 87
Myoporum laetum 56
Myosotis 122
   lyallii 121
   pulvinaris 121
   pygmaea var *drucei* 56
   rakiura 89
Myriophyllum propinquum 33
   robustum 10, 87
   triphyllum 33
Myrsine 57, 61
   australis 36, 97
   divaricata 97
Mystacina 43

Nancy Sound 82
Nannochorista philpotti 117
Neale Burn 30
Nee Islands 81
Nelson 13, *101*
Neomyrtus pedunculata 97
Neothyris lenticularis 79
Nephroma australe 96
Nertera 61
Nestor meridionalis *see* kaka, South Is.
   notabilis *see* kea
ngaio 56
Ngatimamoe Peak *25*
ngiru-ngiru 52
Nothofagus fusca *see* beech, red
   menziesii *see* beech, silver
   solandri var *cliffortioides* *see* beech,
   mountain
Notonemoura spinosa 105
Notoreas 69, *103*, 113
   chioneres 122-123
   galaxias 13, *69*, 123
   hexaleuca 69
   mechanitis 69
   new species *69*, 103
   niphocrena 69
Notosaria nigricans 79

Odonata 44
ÖG3 85
Oho Creek *27*
Olearia 10
   arborescens 36
   bullata *40*, *48*, 113
   colensoi 97, 115
   crosby-smithiana 99
   cymbifolia 121
   ilicifolia 115
   lyallii 89
   moschata 60, *112*, 121
   nummulariifolia 113-14
   oporina 10, 11, 84, *85*, 87, *88*
Oligosoma 86
   acrinasum 85-6, *86*
   chloronoton 86
   inconspicuum 86
   nigriplantare 86
   nigriplantare polychroma 86
Oliver Point 82
Ooperipetallus nanus 114
   viridimaculatus *114*
Orbell, Dr Geoffrey 66
Orbell, Lake *52*
orca 80
Orcinus orca 80
Oreobolus pectinatus 46, 115, 121
Oreostylidium subulatum 45
Orepuki 117
Orocrambus clarkei eximia 68
   scutatus 117

   thymiastes 44
Orophora unicolor 123
Otiran Glaciation 25
Ourisia caespitosa 57, 113
   crosbyi 57, 114
   macrocarpa 57
   remotifolia 57
Outer Gilbert Islands 85
oyster-catcher, South Island pied 83
   variable 83, 90

Pachyptila turtur *see* prion, fairy
Pachyptila vittata *see* prion, broad-billed
Pacific Plate 22
Paget Passage 83
papango *123*
Paprides dugdali 116
Parahebe brevistylus 99
   macrantha var *macrantha* 61
   new species 112
parakeet, orange-fronted 106
   red-crowned 91, 106
   yellow-crowned 40, 91, 106, *117*
Paranephrops zelandicus 117
Paranotoreas brephosata 69
   opipara 69
   zopyra 69
parara 82, 90
Paulina, Mt *121*
Pearl Harbour 28
pekapeka 43
Pelecanoides urinatrix *see* petrel,
   common diving
Pembroke, Mt 50
penguin, blue 11, 82, 90
   Fiordland crested *9*, 12, 82, *83*, 90
Peraxilla colensoi 96, *117*
   tetrapetala 96
perch, butterfly 128
Percnodaimon merula 68, 113
peripatus *114*
petrel, common diving 90
   mottled 12, 82, 83, 90, *95*
Petroica australis *see* robin, South Island
Phalacrocorax carbo *see* shag, black
   melanoleucos *see* shag, little
Philesturnus carunculatus carunculatus
   see saddleback, South Island
Philorheithrus lacustris *104*
Philpott, Alfred 117
Phormium cookianum 115
Phocarctos hookeri *see* sea lion, Hooker's
Phyllachne colensoi 61, 112, 121
Phyllocladus alpinus *40*, 58, 97, 114,
   121
Pigeon Island 126
pigeon, NZ 56, 91, 97, 106, 117
pigeonwood 87
Pimelea 61
   crosby-smithiana 99

gnidia 87
    lyallii 13, 56, 87
    oreophila 48
    prostrata 49, 56
    traversii 122
pine, bog 44-5, 47, 49, *49*
    pink *93*, 97, 114
    pygmy 47, 116
    silver 47
    yellow-silver 47, 96-7
pineapple shrub *61*
pingao *50*, 55-6, *89*, 126-7
piopio, South Island 11
pipipi 42, 107
Pittosporum crassicaule 54
    obcordatum 10, 100
    tenuifolium 36
piupiu 97, *115*
Plagianthus divaricatus 88
Planotortix flammea 103
Plutellus stewartensi 117
plutonic *18*
Poa 55
    astonii 89
    foliosa 89
Podiceps cristatus australis see grebe,
    Australasian crested
Podocarpus 61
    hallii 36, 97
    nivalis 113, 121
Pohlia cf *camptotrachela* 115
Poison Bay *1, 50*, 74, 106
pokotiwha 90
Polysiphonia brodiaei 129
Polystichum cystostegia 60
Pomona Island 36
popokatea 42
Porphyrio mantelli hochstetteri see takahe
    melanotus see pukeko
Port Craig *23, 127*
Poseidon Valley 107
Potamogeton suboblongus 47
Poteriteri, Lake 19, 30, 95
Pourakino River 114
Powelliphanta 68, *73*
    fiordlandica 73
    spedeni 13, 70, 73
Pratia 61
Preservation Inlet 16, 18, 72, 74, 83,
    87, *89*, 92-3, *93*, 106
prion, broad-billed 82, 90
    fairy 90
Procordulia smithii 44
Prodontria setosa 103
Proteodes 104
    carnifex 34, *104*
    clarkei 103, *104*
    smithi 104
Prototroctes oxyrhynchus 39
Prumnopitys ferruginea 97

Pseudaneitea 73
Pseudocoremia berylia 117
Pseudocyphellaria coronata 96
Pseudopanax colensoi 36
    crassifolius 36, 97
    lineare 54
    simplex 97
Psilochorema embersoni 104
Psoroma leprolomum 96
Psychrophila (Caltha) obtusa 57
Pterodroma inexpecta see petrel, mottled
Pteronemobius bigelowi 49
Ptychomnion densifolium 115
Puffinus griseus see shearwater, sooty
pukeko 45, 66
punui *91*
Purser, Lake *27*
puteketeke 36
Puysegur Point 14, 23, 72, *93*, 95
Puysegur Trench 22
Pyrgotis consentiens 103

rail, banded 91
rainfall 14
Rallus philippensis assimilis see rail,
    banded
Ranunculus 10
    acaulis 56, *100*
    buchananii 101
    lyallii 57, 60, *61*
    recens var *lacustris* 33
    sericophyllus 57
Raoulia buchananii 61, 121
    grandiflora 69
rat, brown 124
    Norway 85
    ship 124
rata, southern *1, 9*, 36, *50*, 87, *93*, 97
Rattus exulans 124
    norvegicus 85, 124
    rattus 124
Red Hills *121*
Red Mountain 22
Redcliff *125*
Redcliff Creek 113
remuremu 88
rerewai 47
Resolution 11
Resolution Island 73, *75*, 79, 84, 126
Rhopalimorpha alpina 13
Rhynchodes ursus 104
Rhyssa persuasoria 70
ribbonwood, saltmarsh 88
Richmond, Mt 120
rifleman, South Island 11-12, 40, 52,
    106, 117
rimu 36, 96, 97
riroriro 52
robin, South Island 11, 40, 85, 106-7,
    107, 117, 126

rohutu 97
Romna bicolor 68
Rona Island 36
Rowallan Forest 130
rush, jointed *32*, 36
    wire *40*, 44, 47, 103, 115-16
Rytidosperma setifolium 59, *59*

saddleback, South Island 85, 124
salmo salar 39
salmon, Atlantic 39
Samolus repens 88
sand convolvulus 56
sand daphne 13, 56
sand spurge (milkweed) 56, 89
sandfly 11, 71, *71*
Sand Hill Point *127*
Sargassum verruculosum 129
Save Manapouri Campaign 28, 36
scaup, NZ 36, 44, 55, 108, *123*
Schoenus pauciflorus 121
Scleranthus uniflorus 56
Scoparia subita 117
scorpionfly 117
scurvy grass, Cook's 89
Scythris nigra 49
Scythrodes squalidus 113
sea lion, Hooker's 80
sea perch 78
sea primrose 88
Seaforth catchment *64*, 108
Seaforth River 39, 126
seal, elephant 80
    NZ fur 11, 80
Sealers Beach *127*
Secretary Island 74, 84, 87, 132
sedge 44
sedge, comb 115, 121
Selleria radicans 88
Shag Islands 83
shag, black 36, 44, *123*
    little 36, 44
    pied 82
Shallow Bay 28, *29, 35*
shearwater, sooty 12, *82*, 90
shelduck, paradise 36, 40, 44, 108
Shelter Islands 85
shield bug 113
Shirley Falls 76
shore geranuim 56
shoveler, NZ 44, 108
Sigaus australis 103
    campestris 116
    obelisci 68, *103, 112*, 113, 122
silvereye 12, 52, 91, 106, 117
Sinbad Gully 107
skink, Fiordland 85-6, *86*, 124
skua, brown 82, *90*
slug, giant 70, 73, *73*
smelt, Stokell's 39

snail, giant 68, 70, *73*
    land 12-13, 103
snow grass 102
snow-patch grass 100
snowberry 49
Snowdon Forest 129
Snowdon Peak 118, 120-21
Solander Islands 80, 83, 85, 89-91, *91*,
    132
Solander, Dr Daniel 91
Sophora microphyllum 35
Spaniocerca longicauda 117
speargrass *12*
Spence Burn *112*
Spence Peak 110, *112*
Spey catchment *64*
Sphagnum 44, 121
    australe 115
    cristatum 40, 44
    falcatulum 44
Spit Island *89*
Sprengelia incarnata 88
Stellaria roughii 112, 121
Stenoperla 43
    maclellani 68
Sterna striata 90
Stewart Island 13
Stilbocarpa 13, 72
    lyallii 87, 89, *91*
    robusta 89
Stirling Falls *15*, 76
stoat 42
Stokell, Gerald 39
Stokellia anisodon 39
stonefly *see* stoner
stoner 43, 68, 105, 117
    giant 70, 105
Strigops habroptilis see kakapo
Stripe Point 50
Stuart Mountains 12, 67
sundew *40*
Sutherland Falls 50
Sutherland Sound 76
swan, black 55
Syme, Mt *58*

Takahe Valley 32, *52*, 55, 58, 67, *102*
takahe *9*, 12, 52, *52*, 64, 66-7, *67*
takapu 90
Takitimu Mountains 9, 13, 18, 30, 38,
    46, 61, *69*, 100, 102-3, 110-12, *110*,
    111, 114, 117, 127
tara 90
tarakihi 78
tarapunga 90
tauhou 52
tawhai 54
Tawhitia glaucophanes 113
Te Ana-au Caves 20
Te Anau 126

Te Anau Basin 26, 44, 46-8
Te Anau catchment 40
Te Anau, Lake *11*, 20, *20*, 28, 30, 32-4,
    33, 38, 39, 44, 52, 53, 74, 106, *114*,
    124, 127-8
Te Au, Lake 30
Te Awaatu Channel 76, *132*
Te Oneroa 87
Te Waewae Bay 23, *23*, 30, *45*, 94, 109
Teal Bay *23*
teal, brown *108*
    grey 44
Terebratella sanguinea 78-9
tern, white-fronted 90
Tetrachondra hamiltonii 34
Thompson Sound 74
Thomson Mountains 30
three-finger 36, 87
Tiphobiosis childi 68
    fulva 68
    salmoni 68, 104
titi 12, 90
titi wainui 90
titipounamu 52, 106
toatoa, mountain *40*, 58, 97, 114, 121
toetoe 40
tomtit, South Island 12, 52, 91, 106,
    117
toreapango 90
torrentfish 39, 113
totara 130
    Hall's 36, 97
    snow 113, 121
toutouwai 107
Tower Peak 127
Transit Beach 127
Triglochin striata 88
Tuatapere 28
tube anemone *78*
tui 106, 107, 117
Tunnel Burn 32
turpentine shrub 44, 113
Turret Range 105
Tursiops truncatus see dolphin,
    bottlenose
tussock, blue *47*
    copper *30*, 44, 48, *48, 119*
    sand 56
    silver *47*
Tutoko Valley 72
Tutoko, Mt 27, *27*, 50, *55*

ultramafic *22*, 120, 121
Ulva species 77
Uncinia aucklandica 87
upokororo 39
Upukerora River 39, 120
Uropetala carovei 45
    chiltoni 45
Urtica australis 87

Usnea 96
    capillacea 96
Utricularia monanthos 46

velvetworm 114
Vesicaperla dugdalei 105
volcanism 110

Wahlenbergia congesta 56
Waiau Basin 26, 45
Waiau River 28, *29*, 30, 39, 47, 110, 113,
    118, *125*, 130
Waimeamea River 114
Wairaki Island 84-5
Wairaurahiri River *97, 99*
Waitutu 9, 18, 23, 95, *97, 99*, 107, 131-2
    Forest 12, *97*, 103-4, 130
    River 19, 95
Wakatipu, Lake 30
warbler, grey 12, 52, 91, 106, 117
wasp, giant 70
weevil 124
    bear *104*
    chunky *104*
    giant 70, 72, 114, 122
    knobbled 72, 85, *85*
weka 91, 126
    Stewart Island 90
    western *11, 13*, 64
West Arm 9, 28, 65
West Cape 9, 92-4, *93, 130*
West Dome *121*
Wet Jacket Arm 64
weta, giant 70
    scree 112-13, *112*
    tree 68
wheki 97
whitehead 42
Whitestone River 120
Wilderness Scientific Reserve, The 26,
    49, *49*, 127
Wilmot Pass 9, 94, 105, 127
Wolf River *73*
Woodlaw Forest 130
World Heritage Area 9, 13, 56
wren, rock 12, 52, 64, *64*
    South Island bush 11, 64

Xanthocnemis zealandica 44
Xenicus gilviventris see wren, rock

Yates Point 87
yellowhead 12, 40, 42, 106-7, *117*, 124,
    126, 130

Zelandobius brevicauda 105
    dugdalei 68, *68*, 105
Zelandoperla denticulata 105
Zelandopsyche ingens 68, 70
Zelandosandrus fiordensis 87